The Social Sciences Since the Second World War

ISSUES IN CONTEMPORARY CIVILIZATION

The Social Sciences Since the Second World War

DANIEL BELL

Transaction Books
New Brunswick (U.S.A.) and London (U.K.)

New material this edition copyright © 1982 by Transaction, Inc., New Brunswick, New Jersey 08903. Parts I and II were originally published in *The Great Ideas Today 1979, 1980*. Copyright © 1979, 1980 by Encyclopedia Britannica, Inc. Reprinted by permission.

Library of Congress Catalog Number: 80-27957
ISBN: 0-87855-426-2 (cloth), 0-87855-872-1 (paper)
Printed in the United States of America

Library of Congress Cataloging in Publication Data
Bell, Daniel.
    The social sciences since the Second World War.

    (Issues in contemporary civilization)
    "Originally appeared in two parts in the Encyclopedia Britannica's Great ideas today series."
    1. Social sciences. I. Title.
H61.B455   300'.9'04   80-27957
ISBN 0-87855-426-2
ISBN 0-87855-872-1 (pbk.)

For Robert K. Merton
magister ludi

Contents

Introduction to the
Transaction Books Edition

In 1830, at age thirty-two, Auguste Comte, a man of monomaniacal genius (four years earlier, after a nervous breakdown, he had signed his marriage papers as "Brutus Bonaparte Comte") began the publication in six volumes of the monumental *Cours de philosophie positive*. This task, completed in 1842, sought to set forth in comprehensive outline the unity of human knowledge.* Comte's intention was not to produce an encyclopedia or a detailed account of the sciences—that "would be endless and would require a scientific preparation as no one man possesses," he wrote (p. 31). Rather, he sought to exhibit a principle of classification and to demonstrate a unity of the sciences through their exemplification in the "positive method."

For Comte, to use a modern idiom, all phenomena, natural and social, have a constitutive structure, an intrinsic order which it was the task of science, through the positive method, to discern. As he wrote:

> . . . it is our business to contemplate order, that we may perfect it; and not to create it; which would be impossible. In a scientific view, this master-thought of *universal social interconnection* becomes the consequence and complement of a fundamental idea . . . . [W]herever there is any system whatever a certain interconnection must exist. The purely mechanical phenomena of astronomy offer the first suggestion of it. . . . But the relation becomes closer and more marked in proportion to the complexity and diminished generality of the phenomena and thus it is, in organic systems

---

*An edition in English, freely translated and condensed by Harriet Martineau, was published in two volumes in London, in 1853, and the two were combined in a single volume published in New York, in 1856. Miss Martineau's compressions were largely in the sections on Mathematics, Astronomy and Physics (which had been vetted by a Professor Nichol of Glasgow). Of the some 800 pages in the English version, about half were devoted to "social physics," Comte's overall term for the social sciences. All page citations in this Introduction are taken from the 1856 edition.

that we must look for the fullest mutual connection.... The idea must therefore be scientifically preponderant in social physics even more than in biology.... Its consideration is, in fact, as indispensable in assigning its encyclopediac rank to social science as ... in instituting Social Physics a science at all. (pp. 461-462, italics added)*

Sociology was to be the queen of the sciences:

> ... when the action of man upon nature is duly systematized under the new body of doctrine, it must be done under the guidance of sociological philosophy, which alone is able to combine all the scientific aspects requisite for the great work.... When sociological theory has once reached the positive state, there is nothing except the opposition of the ignorant and the interested [i.e., the vested interests] to prevent the human view from resuming its natural place at the head of all human speculation. (pp. 795-796; 794).

Comte's synoptic vision was based on three considerations: that "all phenomena are subjected to invariable natural Laws"; that these laws are discernible through the methods of science, inductive and deductive; and that the evolution of human thought from the theological to the metaphysical to the positive demonstrated the unfolding of knowledge so that a new threshold of reality was now unveiled.

This search for a unifying leitmotif has been the hallmark of the grand sages of sociology. Herbert Spencer, that "dogmatist of genius" whose life overlapped Comte's and whose theories paralleled Comte's, proclaimed his credo:

> The law of organic progress is the law of all progress. Whether it be the development of the Earth, in the development of Life upon its surface, in the development of Society, of Government, of Manufacture, of Commerce, of Language, Literature, Science, Art, this same evolution of the simple into the complex through successive differentiations holds throughout. From the earliest traceable cosmical changes down to the latest results of civilization, we shall find that the transformation of the homogeneous into the heterogeneous is that in which progress essentially consists.

In that towering facade, *The Principles of Sociology* (whose construction took two decades, from 1876 to 1896, to complete), Spencer sought to demonstrate that all social phenomena—in particular the tendency of social arrangements to come into stable equillibrium—conform to invariant laws.†

---

*Is it too much to suggest that this distinction of Comte is the basis for Durkheim's usage of "mechanical" and "organic" solidarity, as a movement from simpler to more complex forms?

†There is a magisterial intellectual biography of Spencer by J.Y.D. Peel, *Herbert Spencer: the evolution of a sociologist* (New York: Basic Books, 1971), and a fine, if unfortunately forgotten, study by Jay Rumney, *Herbert Spencer's Sociology*, published in 1937, reprinted in paperback by Atherton Press, New York, 1966.

Lester F. Ward (1841–1913), called "the American Aristotle" by an admiring acolyte, created his own system using the idea of synergy—a term that he coined from the synthesis of energy and mutuality—to explain the evolution of structures from the simple to the complex through the antithetical—in the cant phrase of the day one would say dialectical—forces of nature. Ward had been a botanist and a paleontologist, and he grafted onto sociology a biological language (which is why he may have been mistaken for Aristotle), such as *kariokinesis*, for the historical processes of social differentiation (as in cells); and *sympoidal development*, in which successive branches become the main stem, leaving the original ones as vanishing vestiges, for the processes of colonization.

Portentous and prolific, Ward impressed the other autodidacts of his time as a speculative genius. Yet it is only the parochialism of early American sociology that finds any originality in Ward. His sociology is a template of Comte, whom he read along with Haeckel and Spencer, and his classification of the sciences, which he regarded as the foundation of his system (e.g., astronomy as "the most general and least complex" of the sciences and sociology as "the least general and most complex" of the sciences), is a mindless repetition of Comte. It may be said, perhaps unkindly, that Ward has vanished without a vestige.*

In the twentieth century, the social sciences moved away from these large, sweeping historical generalizations and the building of chambered ziggurats. In theory, the social sciences became ahistorical and analytical; in detail, they became empirical; and in method, largely quantitative.

The move to an analytical mode had long been evident in economics—a term that was not established until it was used by Alfred Mar-

---

*It should be pointed out that Ward had another claim to fame, an extraordinary one that has been largely overlooked by the historians of eccentric intellectual ideas. As one of his expositors points out:

> Lester F. Ward was a thinker of the first rank, to be classed with Marx, Freud, and Einstein. He stands beside these men because, like them, during a lifetime of vigorous intellectual work, he achieved one tremendous and comparatively unanswerable generalization which has permanently enriched man's thought thereafter.... *Ward, for the first time, solved the problem of the origin and development of the sexes*. It is for this that the future will remember him, rather than for his tremendous structure of sociological thinking or his brilliant judgment upon a thousand minor aspects of social relationships. (emphasis added)

According to Ward, sexual mating originated at about the stage of the barnacles, by the female developing separate males on her own body, from which she selected her mate or mates. As his admirer complains about the neglect of this idea:

> When it is realized that sexual union thus originated in the mating of the mother with her offspring-husband, and this is compared with Freud's emphasis on the mother-son relationship, the Oedipus complex, the omitted importance of Ward in the Freudian system, as a scientific buttress for the psychoanalytic structure, is easily seen (Clement Wood, *The Sociology of Lester F. Ward*, New York: Vanguard Press, 1930, pp. xi, xiv).

Alas, Freudian thought may have its own barnacles, but not those of Lester F. Ward.

shall in 1890 in his *Principles*. Economics before Adam Smith had been "moral philosophy," concerned with the rules of proper household management in the tradition of Aristotle's *Politics*. From Smith to Mill it had been "political economy," concerned with the creation of wealth within the framework of the polity. After Marshall, economics became an ahistorical "analytical engine," intent (following the example of classical mechanics) on setting forth basic relationships (e.g., supply and demand, investment and consumption, indifference curves and opportunity costs) which, when given quantitative magnitudes, would provide the coefficients of invariance that would be applicable as a set of economizing techniques to all choice and scarcity situations. In sociology, as in the work of Tönnies, Weber, and Durkheim, the intention was to eschew evolution (though the concepts were embedded in an evolutionary frame) and to define the basic types of social structures that would allow the sociologist to compare any set of societies and kinds of social actions. In anthropology there was, again, the move away from history and evolution (or the study of comparative, though isolated, traits), to functional analysis and the integration of social structures and cultures, as in the work of Malinowski and Radcliffe-Brown.

In research, the change was away from speculative generalization to data collection, case studies, surveys, and participant observation, such as the pioneering studies of the business cycle initiated by Wesley Clair Mitchell and his students; the life-histories of immigrants, such as *The Polish Peasant in Europe and America*, by W.I. Thomas and Florian Znaniecki; and the anthropological field studies initiated by Franz Boas and his students. In methodology there was the extraordinary elaboration of statistical techniques for the manipulation of the relation between variables from the work of Karl Pearson and R.A. Fisher to the formalization of models through mathematical representations. Table 1, "Basic Innovations in Social Science, 1900–65," by Karl Deutsch and his associates, which is reproduced at the beginning of this monograph, documents in dramatic fashion the emergent centrality of that quantitative emphasis.

Given that extraordinary upsurge in the social sciences, an efflorescence which some writers, perhaps rashly, have likened to the triumphal consolidation of physics in the seventeenth century, the question naturally has arisen: what have we learned from all this? Not in the details, for these have been enormous, but in some synoptic or coherent bodies of new knowledge that constitute an advance on the past: in some sets of verified generalizations about human behavior or social relationships; in some body of techniques or methodologies to apply that knowledge for social design or social purposes; in some synthetic theories to order this knowledge in a comprehensive way and relate these discoveries to previous bodies of knowledge or—dare the thought—to the "perennial wisdom" embodied in the classic summations of human experience. To put the question grandly: if physics and

its allied sciences have given us a greater and more complex understanding of nature so that we have been able to transform nature, what
have the social sciences learned about human nature and the social
structures that people create, which is more than the generalizations of
the great philosophers and which would enable us to achieve the utopian visions of our forebears? Or, to put the issue in the vernacular: if
we have been able to engineer $E=MC^2$ into a nuclear bomb, and to put
a man on the moon, can we educate our children better, design a more
pleasing environment, utilize productivity to conquer poverty, or
create an "artificial intelligence" that would extend men's powers to
think, as machines have extended our physical powers? In the mid-
twentieth century these were promises. Have those promises been
realized?

This, in short, was the assignment given me by the editors of *The
Great Ideas Today*, that enterprise of the Encyclopedia Britannica
which published the *Syntopicon* of Mortimer Adler, a cross-indexed
analytical guide to the "great ideas" formulated by the master-
thinkers of the human imagination; and the Great Books of the Western World which embody those ideas. Each year, the editors of *The
Great Ideas Today* publish a yearbook which focuses attention on some
major intellectual or policy issue, renews current developments in the
arts and sciences, examines the status of a "great idea," and publishes
an addition to the Great Books library. I was asked to review the social
sciences since the end of the Second World War. My essay, divided in
two parts, appeared in the 1979 and 1980 volumes of *The Great Ideas
Today*. Thanks to the generosity of its editors, in particular John Van
Doren, the executive editor, and the initiative of Transaction Books
and its president, Irving Louis Horowitz, that essay appears here as an
independent publication for a social-science audience.

An essay speaks for itself and I shall not rehearse its contents here.
Yet it might be useful for the reader to know what this essay is not, and
to illustrate what has been omitted.

This is not a detailed review of the social sciences by disciplines.
Though there is a considerable discussion of economics, I do so because
that discipline has made the largest claims to establishing—in the
neoclassical paradigm from Alfred Marshall to Paul Samuelson—a coherent view of "rational" behavior in the allocation of goods and services, and to press that claim on the formulation of public policy; it is
not a review of the field itself. Nor do I deal with the large number of
important individual social-science works that have made a mark, or
with the large number of new techniques and methodologies. My emphasis is on those synoptic efforts to provide a systematic body of theory—whether as an intention, as in artificial intelligence and cognitive
modelling; or an interdisciplinary approach, as in culture and personality; or a major new perspective, as with sociobiology or structural-

ism—which set forth some coherent statement about human behavior or social structure.

Thus, I have slighted important individual studies, such as those by Samuel Stouffer and his associates in *The American Soldier*, which pioneered both in methodology and in their use of a strategic concept such as "relative deprivation"; the work of Paul Lazarsfeld and his associates in studying voting behavior and communication, with its close attention to the "why of decision," and the role of personal influence; or the work of Robert Merton, both in his programmatic efforts to codify theory and research and, with his associates, in his substantive work in the sociology of science.

The question of borderlines always arises, particularly where new approaches derive from a seminal work, as in the instance of the *Theory of Games and Economic Behavior*, by John von Neumann and Oskar Morgenstern (Princeton, 1944). What today would be called "game theory," and more broadly "decision theory," has had some brilliant practitioners. An influential book, summarizing work to that date, was that of Duncan Luce and Howard Raiffa, *Games and Decisions* (Wiley, 1958). But in the twenty years since that codification, game theory and decision theory have splayed out into such diverse areas as microeconomics, administrative behavior, command and control theory, and international strategy. Some brilliant books have been produced, such as Thomas Schelling's on *The Strategy of Conflict*. The mode of analysis has proliferated and become absorbed into many diverse fields and academic curricula. But the initial promise of a comprehensive theory which would, like Machiavelli's *The Prince,* codify—and then formalize—propositions about strategy, has not materialized. It remains an approach.

A different kind of "borderline area" is the rising attention to semiotics, as a generic term for the interest in systems of signs, symbols, and meanings. Semiotics has a long history in philosophy, beginning with the work of Charles Peirce, who coined the term for a general theory of signs, and continuing later with the work of Saussure, who used the term semiology to designate language as a constructed system of relations. While the themes have become central for literary studies and hermeneutics, it has been only in the 1970s that symbolism and semiotics have become a major feature of social-science studies, especially in anthropology, in the work of Clifford Geertz (who calls it "interpretative anthropology") and Mary Douglas and Victor Turner (who calls it symbology). One can say that semiotics is an interest, a technique of exploration, even a field (dealing with systems of symbols and meanings), yet it lacks the unified focus of structuralism and becomes, in some instances, almost coterminous with a theory of culture.*

---

*For a general summary, see Thomas A. Sebeok, editor, *Sight, Sound and Sense* (Bloomington: Indiana University Press, 1978), especially the essay by Milton Singer, "For a Semiotic Anthropology," pp. 202-231.

I have almost entirely omitted the sprawling area of political science, not because of its sprawl but because even when some efforts have been made to create new perspectives and paradigms—I think of the concept of "political culture," initiated by Gabriel Almond, Lucien Pye, and Sidney Verba; of "systems analysis," such as that of David Easton; the "economic approach" to politics, such as that of Anthony Downs; or the intriguing work on "collective choice," by Mancur Olson, John Harsanyi, and Tullock and Buchanan—these have lacked the larger synthetic breadth of the movements and schools that I have discussed.

Within the broad field of politics, I do regret one neglect, the efforts to establish a new normative foundation for political philosophy as represented in the work of John Rawls in his *A Theory of Justice* (Harvard University Press, 1971). What makes that book distinctive is not only the fresh effort to deal with the issues of "distributive justice," issues that Marxian and utopian theories thought would vanish under socialism and "abundance," but in doing so Rawls combines the rigor of analytic philosophy with the theorems of welfare economics, in particular those of Amartya Sen.*

My reason for this neglect was a self-denying ordinance against incursions into philosophy—with one crucial exception noted below—and into the equally large literature on the epistemological foundations of the social sciences (e.g., the writings of Peter Winch, Ernest Gellner, W.G. Runciman, Anthony Giddens, Alasdair MacIntyre, et al.). For the same reason I have slighted the thinking of the phenomenologists who follow Edmund Husserl, namely Merleau-Ponty, Alfred Schutz, and the exotic offshoot in sociology called ethnomethodology.

About the resurgence of neo-Marxism one could write an essay as lengthy as the present one, if not longer; after all, it is not only a science but a scholasticism, and any such doctrinal efforts related to a "sacred text" multiply their schisms endlessly. What is striking is that, at this date, one finds Marxist writers still quarrelling about the definition of "modes of production," "social formation," and even the boundary definitions of such axial terms as "working class" and "proletariat." The reason is that on all the concepts associated with the name of Marx—alienation, ideology, the theory of class, historical materialism (a term he never used but which was coined by Engels), dialectical materialism (a term that neither Marx nor Engels used but which was minted by the Russian Marxist Georgi Plekhanov)—there is *no single unambiguous definition* by Marx of any of these concepts. So, in recent years there has been an endless debate within the Marxist camp on the extent of the "positivist" Engelian revision of the early Marx, whether there is a sustained continuity in the thinking of Marx between his

---

*For some useful discussions, see *Philosophy and Economic Theory*, edited by Frank Hahn and Martin Hollis (Oxford University Press, 1977), especially the essay by Armatya Sen entitled "Rational Fools," and the symposium, *Reading Rawls*, edited by Norman Daniels (Oxford: Blackwell, 1975).

earlier philosophical writings and his later economic studies, and so on. And this is tiresome for the general reader.

There are three areas where neo-Marxist writing—and it is quite striking that almost all this has taken place outside the Soviet Union and the Communist world where Marxian theory has petrified—has dealt with substantive questions. One is a theory of the State, the second an attempt to resolve the ambiguities of the Marxian theory of value, and third the relation of culture to politics.

Classical Marxism never had a theory of "the State." It did not because all political divisions were seen, basically, as reflections of underlying societal (i.e., class) divisions. In that broad sense, politics, like ideology and culture, was epiphenomenal, directly or indirectly "reflecting" the basic class divisions. "The State" was seen as the simple instrument of the ruling class. Marx's most brilliant individual essay, *The Eighteenth Brumaire of Louis Napoleon*, had to wrestle with the "test case" that threatened to "falsify" the theory: how to explain that an adventurer representing no single class, using the *jeunesse doré* and the *lumpenproletariat* of Paris, could win power in a plebiscitary election and maintain power by manipulating one class against another. In explaining the role of Louis Napoleon, Marx emphasized the distinction between politics, which could reflect the diverse interests of "fractions" of classes, and the "underlying" material system. It was a distinction that Trotsky sought to use in *The Revolution Betrayed* (1937) to explain the role of Stalin (whom he likened to Louis Napoleon) in holding political power while the "underlying" system itself was socialist.

The question of the "autonomy of politics," and the independent role of a State over and above individual capitalist groups, or even of capitalists to save capitalism, is a theme that has preoccupied neo-Marxist writers, such as Ralph Miliband and Nicos Poulantzis. What is striking in their work is the lack of any empirical or historical study, so that the "debates" become essentially textual and scholastic. Other than the writings of neo-Trotskyite theorists (from the late Max Schactman to Ernest Mandel), there has been little examination of the role of the State in the Communist world itself.*

Among Marxian economists, there have been many efforts to resolve the thorny question of the "labor theory of value," and the disjunction of "value" and "price." Following the publication of Piero Sraffa's *Production of Commodities by Means of Commodities* (Cambridge, 1960), a number of economists such as Michio Morishima and Ian Steedman (e.g., *Marx After Sraffa*, London, 1977) have sought a way of reestab-

---

*Marxism seems almost to have become a "science" of the capitalist and Western world. Yet in what way could Marxist theory explain the Gulag inside the Soviet Union; the death camps of Cambodia; the intense ideological and political rivalry between the Soviet Union and Communist China; the antagonism and outright war between Vietnam and Cambodia, a few years back close allies against Western "imperialism."

lishing Marxian economics without its "metaphysical baggage." These, however, are technical and mathematical and defy easy exposition.*

In the third area, on the relation of culture to politics, the most significant development was the "rediscovery" of the writings of the Italian communist leader Antonio Gramsci, a one-time student of Benedetto Croce, who died in 1937 in a Fascist prison. Gramsci's central theme was the idea of "hegemony," or the way in which the dominant ideas of the time reflected the dominant class and shaped the sociological and cultural discourse in a society. In that respect, the cultural domain was reestablished as a major area of ideological conflict, and the intellectual, as the bearer of ideologies, reinstated as a significant figure. A vulgar Marxist might say that the theory is a self-serving ideology for intellectuals who do not want to subordinate themselves to a working class; a non-Marxist vulgarian might observe that the society where "hegemony" rules in a singular way is the Soviet Union— but that little of Gramsci's analysis has been applied to that society.

The major debates in neo-Marxism, however, have derived from social philosophy, and these have been exemplified in such writers as Georg Lukács, Jean-Paul Sartre, Louis Althusser, and Max Horkheimer and T.W. Adorno, the heads of the so-called Frankfurt School. Since the central world-views that Marxism seeks to present—the relation of theory to practice, of critical Reason and History—rests on these philosophical debates, the discussion of neo-Marxism in this essay has been primarily of these philosophers.

The original hope of August Comte was to present a unified view of man's knowledge through the unity of science, as Aristotle two thousand years before had presented a view of the unity of man and nature through the concept of entelechy (the realized design of form and material responsive to a natural end), and the organon of logic. The hope is a recurrent one. One of the most recent major efforts (1939–69) was that of Otto Neurath, Rudolf Carnap, and Charles Morris to bring forth an *Encyclopedia of Unified Science*, though it is ironic that one of the monographs in that series, *The Structure of Scientific Revolutions*, by Thomas Kuhn, with his notion of disjunctive paradigms, has probably done more (though unfairly to the intentions of the author) to introduce a relativism in the philosophy of science than any other work in the contemporary history of science. By and large, however, not only have such hopes not been realized, but there is a sense today that we are probably farther from that ambition than at most times in our intellectual history. Some of the reasons have been

---

* For a fluent, but critical, review of Marxian theory in the light of these efforts, see, Mark Blaug, *A Methodological Appraisal of Marxian Economics* (North Holland Publishing Co., 1980).

suggested in this review of some partial efforts and approaches. The larger reason lies in some epistemological dilemmas which are beyond the scope of this essay.*

The questions that are before us are the questions that go back to the very origin of the rise of philosophy. Can we assume a "unity of nature"? Are Man and Society subsumed under a natural order, their "natures" to be discerned in underlying uniformities or invariant actions? Few philosophers are sure of their answers. We are now at a hiatus. The repudiation of positivism, the "historicizing" of the philosophy of science, the rise of relativism, the loss of faith in the Future or History as the standpoint of "Reason" from which to evaluate the present, the new interest in "interpretative" social science, with its emphasis on symbolism and meaning rather than causality and general theory,† all bespeak the clearing of the major intellectual positions that have undergirded social theory. And there is little agreement as to new directions. This is for some the dismaying, and for others the cheering, news about the social sciences since the Second World War. It has been said that optimism is a philosophy and pessimism a character trait; the reader will have to take his stand.

One of the pleasures of an author is the deed of dedication, which is at the same time a gesture of homage and an act of identification. For anyone who has known him, as a scholar and friend, he is an exemplar. That is why it is a pleasure to dedicate this book about social science, its reach and its grasp, to Robert K. Merton, *magister ludi*.

Cambridge, Mass.
December 1980

---

*Two major efforts to present such reasons are Edmund Husserl's *The Crisis of the European Sciences* (1935), and Jürgen Habermas, *Knowledge and Human Interests* (1971).

†For a useful account of this new development, one with which I would identify, see *Interpretive Social Science: A Reader*, edited by Paul Rabinow and William M. Sullivan (University of California Press, 1979).

Part I

In February 1971 Karl Deutsch of Harvard University and two associates published a study in *Science* magazine listing sixty-two "advances in social science" from 1900 to 1965. Their intention was to study the conditions for "creative success in the social sciences," but to do so, of course, they had to demonstrate that such successes had indeed occurred.

The criterion of achievement was that a theory, or a finding, put forth a "new perception of relationships"; or stipulated verifiable propositions of the "if . . . then" form; or produced "a substantial impact that led to further knowledge." After compiling the list (and checking these judgments with those of individuals in other fields), they concluded:

1. There *are* such things as social science achievements and social inventions, which are almost as clearly defined and as operational as technological achievements and inventions.
2. These achievements have commonly been the result of conscious and systematic research and development efforts by individuals or teams working on particular problems in a small number of interdisciplinary centers.
3. These achievements have had widespread acceptance or major social effects in surprisingly short times; median times are in the range of ten to fifteen years, a range comparable with the median times for widespread acceptance of major technological inventions.[1]

What is striking about the list (*see* Tables 1 and 2) is that the early achievements are quite theoretical and, in the jargon of the field, largely qualitative—such as the theory of bureaucracy associated with Max Weber, or the revolutionary-vanguard role of the mobilized party initiated by V. I. Lenin, or the psychoanalytic and depth psychology of Freud, Jung, and Adler—while the later achievements, or even the later developments of early findings, are (with almost the sole exception of the anthropological structuralism of Claude Lévi-Strauss) primarily innovations of mathematical and statistical techniques, or theories derived from quantitative analysis, such as information theory or growth models in economics. Indeed, as the authors write:

Quantitative problems or findings (or both) characterized two-thirds of all advances, and five-sixths of those were made after 1930 (Table 1, column 7). Completely nonquantitative contributors—the recognition of new patterns without any clear implication of quantitative problems—were rare throughout the period and extremely rare since 1930.

This is, surely, one of the reasons why the social sciences, in the period after 1940, acquired new prestige and influence. With the rapid advance in sophisticated new techniques, particularly after the introduction of the computer, theories were no longer simply ideas or rhetoric but propositions that could be stated in empirical and verifiable form. To use the jargon again, social sciences were becoming "hard," like the natural sciences.

A second factor conjoined. This was the halo effect of science, particularly because of its crucial role in World War II. One need go back only twenty-five more years, to World War I, for an instructive contrast. At that time, Thomas Alva Edison had been appointed head of the Navy consulting board. As his biographer Matthew Josephson tells the story, Edison decided that they ought to have a physicist on the board, because they might need someone to deal with mathematical or statistical questions should they arise; but since the Navy did not have a classification of physicist, the man who was appointed was paid as a chemist. James B. Conant tells a similar story. Conant, before becoming president of Harvard, had been a chemist. At the time of the U.S. entry into World War I, Conant was president of the American Chemical Society. In that capacity he went to Newton D. Baker, then Secretary of War, and offered his services and those of the members of the Society to the war effort. Baker thanked him for his patriotism, told him he would inquire into the need, and when Conant returned a week later, he was told that the services of the Society were unnecessary because the War Department already had a sufficient number of chemists.

During World War II the Manhattan Project produced the atomic bomb; the Radiation Laboratory at MIT developed radar (which had been invented by the British); the need for "number crunching" speeded the development of the electronic computer; and the mobilization of thousands of scientists produced hundreds of new devices for the war effort.

The simple thought occurred to many: if the widespread mobilization of science, and the concentration on some specific objectives, could produce scientific and technological breakthroughs, why could not a similar mobilization—the building of interdisciplinary teams—produce similar results in the social sciences? An example was at hand: the mobilization of the economy for war. The experience of mobilization had produced a wide and varied number of new experiences: the planning for production, the allocation of material, new psychological selection and testing procedures, psychological warfare, studies of the means of maintaining soldier and civilian morale, and dozens of other organized research and managerial efforts. Why could not a sustained effort, underwritten by large-scale expenditures, now advance the social sciences in the way that the natural sciences had

Table 1. Basic Innovations in Social Science, 1900-65

Abbreviations in column 1: An, anthropology; Ec, economics; Math, mathematics; Phil, philosophy, logic, and history of science; Pol, politics; Psy, psychology; Soc, sociology.

Contribution 1	Contributor 2	Time 3	Place 4
1. Theory and measurement of social inequalities (Ec)	V. Pareto C. Gini	1900 1908	Lausanne, Swit. Cagliari, It. Padua, It. Rome, It.
2. Sociology of bureaucracy, culture, and values (Soc)	M. Weber	1900–21	Freiburg, Ger. Heidelberg, Ger. Munich, Ger.
3. Theory of one-party organization and revolution (Pol)	V. I. Lenin	1900–17	Shushenskoe, Siberia London, Eng. Munich, Ger.
4. Psychoanalysis and depth psychology (Psy)	S. Freud C. G. Jung A. Adler	1900–25 1910–30 1910–30	Vienna, Aus.
5. Correlation analysis and social theory (Math)	K. Pearson F. Edgeworth R. A. Fisher	1900–28 1900–30 1920–48	London, Eng. Oxford, Eng. Cambridge, Eng. Harfenden, Eng.
6. Gradual social transformation (Pol)	B. Webb S. Webb G. B. Shaw H. G. Wells	1900–38	London, Eng.
7. Elite studies (Soc)	G. Mosca V. Pareto H. D. Lasswell	1900–23 1900–16 1936–52	Turin, It. Lausanne, Swit. Chicago, Ill.
8. Unity of logic and mathematics (Phil)	B. Russell A. N. Whitehead	1905–14	Cambridge, Eng.
9. Pragmatic and behavioral psychology (Psy)	J. Dewey G. H. Mead C. Cooley W. I. Thomas	1905–25 1900–34 1900–30 1900–40	Ann Arbor, Mich. Chicago, Ill. Ann Arbor, Mich. Chicago, Ill. New York, N.Y.
10. Learning theory (Psy)	E. L. Thorndike C. Hull et al.	1905–40 1929–40	New York, N.Y. New Haven, Conn.
11. Intelligence tests (Psy)	A. Binet L. Terman C. Spearman	1905–11 1916–37 1904–27	Paris, Fr. Stanford, Calif. London, Eng.
12. Role of innovations in socioeconomic change (Ec)	J. A. Schumpeter W. F. Ogburn A. P. Usher J. Schmookler	1908–14 1946–50 1922–30 1924 1966	Vienna, Aus. Cambridge, Mass. New York, N.Y. Cambridge, Mass. Minneapolis, Minn.
13. Conditioned reflexes (Psy)	I. Pavlov	1910–30	Leningrad, U.S.S.R.
14. Gestalt psychology (Psy)	M. Wertheimer K. Koffka W. Koehler	1912–32	Berlin, Ger.
15. Sociometry and sociograms (Soc)	J. L. Moreno	1915 1934–43	Innsbruck, Aus.
16. Soviet type of one-party state (Pol)	V. I. Lenin et al.	1917–21	Leningrad, U.S.S.R.
17. Large-scale nonviolent political action (Pol)	M. K. Gandhi	1918–34	Ahmedabad, India

In column 6, + N indicates a larger number of collaborators with a less crucial share in the work. Abbreviations in column 7: QFE, quantitative findings explicit; QPE, quantitative problems explicit; QPI, quantitative problems implied; Non-Q, predominantly nonquantitative.

Type of support 5	No. of workers 6	Quantitative aspects 7	Years until impact 8
University chairs	1 + N	QFE	25
University chair with research support	1	QPI	20 ± 10
Underground party	1 + N	QPI	10 ± 5
University institute of psychology	1 + N	Non-Q	30 ± 10
University chairs	1 + N	QFE	25 ± 15
Fabian society	4 + N	QPE	35 ± 5
University institutes	1 + N	QFE	40 ± 10
University institute	2	QPE	30
University chairs	1	Non-Q	20 ± 10
Teachers college, Institute of human relations	1 + N	QFE	20 ± 5
Testing organizations	1 + N	QFE	15 ± 5
University chair and research program	1 + N	QPI	40
Imperial medico-surgical academy	1 + N	QPI	20 ± 10
University chairs	3 + N	Non-Q	25 ± 5
University chair	1	QFE	10
Politburo	1 + N	QPI	5 ± 5
Political movement and institute (ashram)	1 + N	Non-Q	15 ± 10

Contribution 1	Contributor 2	Time 3	Place 4
18. Central economic planning (Ec)	Q. Krassin G. Grinko	1920–26	Moscow, U.S.S.R.
19. Social welfare function in politics and economics (Ec)	A. C. Pigou K. Arrow	1920–56 1951	London, Eng. Stanford, Calif.
20. Logical empiricism and unity of science (Phil)	M. Schlick R. Carnap O. Neurath P. Frank L. Wittgenstein H. Reichenbach C. Morris	1921–38 1921 1936–50	Vienna, Aus. Cambridge, Eng. Berlin, Ger. Chicago, Ill. Cambridge, Mass.
21. Quantitative mathematical studies of war (Pol)	L. F. Richardson Q. Wright	1921–55 1936–66	London, Eng. Chicago, Ill.
22. Projective tests (Psy)	H. Rorschach H. Murray	1923	Herisau, Swit. Cambridge, Mass.
23. Sociology of knowledge and science (Soc)	K. Mannheim R. K. Merton D. deS. Price	1923–33 1937 1950–60	Heidelberg, Ger. Frankfurt, Ger. Princeton, N.J. New Haven, Conn.
24. Quantitative political science and basic theory (Pol)	C. Merriam S. Rice H. Gosnell H. D. Lasswell	1925–36	Chicago, Ill.
25. Functionalist anthropology and sociology (An)	A. R. Radcliffe-Brown B. Malinowski T. Parsons	1925 1925–45 1932–50	Cape Town, S. Afr. Sidney, Aus. Chicago, Ill. Oxford, Eng. London, Eng. Cambridge, Mass.
26. Ecosystem theory (Soc)	R. Park E. W. Burgess	1926–38	Chicago, Ill.
27. Factor analysis (Math)	L. Thurstone	1926–48	Chicago, Ill.
28. Operational definitions (Phil)	P. W. Bridgman	1927–38	Cambridge, Mass.
29. Structural linguistics (Math)	R. Jakobson and Prague circle N. Chomsky	1927–67 1957–	Brno, Czech. Cambridge, Mass. Cambridge, Mass.
30. Economic propensities, employment, and fiscal policy (Ec)	J. M. Keynes	1928–44	Cambridge, Eng.
31. Game theory (Math)	J. v. Neumann O. Morgenstern	1928–44 1944–58	Berlin, Ger. Princeton, N.J.
32. Peasant and guerrilla organization and government (Pol)	Mao Tse-tung	1929–49	Kiangsi, P. R. China Yenan, P. R. China Peking, P. R. China
33. Community studies (Soc)	R. Lynd H. Lynd L. Warner C. Kluckhohn	1929–62 1941	New York, N.Y. Chicago, Ill.

Type of support 5	No. of workers 6	Quantitative aspects 7	Years until impact 8
Government institute	1 + N	QFE	7 ± 6
University chairs	1 + N	QPE	40 ± 10
Vienna circle and university chairs	3 + N	QPI	20 ± 5
University chairs			
University chair and research program	1 + N	QFE	25 ± 10
Cantonal mental institute University chair	1	Non-Q	15 ± 5
University chairs, institutes, and programs	1 + N	Non-Q	10
University chairs	3 + N	QFE	15 ± 5
University chairs and travel grants	1 + N	Non-Q	20 ± 10
University chairs	2 + N	QFE	25 ± 5
University chair	1 + N	QFE	15 ± 10
University chair	1	QPI	15 ± 5
University chairs and programs	1 + N	QPE	20 ± 10
University chair	1 + N	QFE	6 ± 4
University chairs and institute	2 + N	QFE	10 ± 5
Political movement	1 + N	QPI	15 ± 10
University chairs	2	QFE	20 ± 5

Contribution 1	Contributor 2	Time 3	Place 4
34. Culture and personality and comparative child rearing (An)	R. Benedict	1930	New York, N.Y.
	M. Mead	1930	
	G. Gorer		
	A. Kardiner	1939	
	J. Piaget	1940–60	Geneva, Swit.
	E. Erikson	1950	Cambridge, Mass.
	J. Whiting	1953	Cambridge, Mass.
	I. Child		New Haven, Conn.
35. Economics of monopolistic competiton (Ec)	E. H. Chamberlin	1930–33	Cambridge, Mass.
	J. Robinson		Cambridge, Eng.
36. Authoritarian personality and family structure (Psy)	M. Horkheimer	1930–32	Frankfurt, Ger.
	H. Marcuse		
	E. Fromm		
	T. Adorno *et al.*	1950	Stanford, Calif.
	A. Mitscherlich	1962	Frankfurt, Ger.
			Heidelberg, Ger.
37. Large-scale sampling in social research (Math)	M. Hansen	1930–53	Washington, D.C.
38. Laboratory study of small groups (Psy)	K. Lewin	1932–36	Cambridge, Mass.
	R. Lippitt		
	R. Likert		
	D. Cartwright		
39. National income accounting (Ec)	S. Kuznets	1933–40	Philadelphia, Pa.
	C. Clark		Cambridge, Eng.
	U.N. Statistical Office	1953	Washington, D.C. New York, N.Y.
40. General systems analysis (Phil)	L. v. Bertalanffy	1936	Vienna, Aus.
	N. Rashevsky		Chicago, Ill.
	J. G. Miller	1956	Ann Arbor, Mich.
	A. Rapoport		
	R. W. Gerard		
	K. Boulding		
41. Attitude survey and opinion polling (Psy)	G. Gallup	1936	Princeton, N.J.
	H. Cantril	1937–52	
	P. F. Lazarsfeld	1940	New York, N.Y.
	A. Campbell	1942	Ann Arbor, Mich.
42. Input-out analysis (Ec)	W. Leontief	1936–53	Cambridge, Mass.
43. Linear programming (Ec)	L. Kantorovich	1938–50	Leningrad, U.S.S.R.
	J. B. Souto	1941	Buenos Aires, Arg.
	G. B. Dantzig	1948	Washington, D.C.
	R. Dorfman	1958	Berkeley, Calif.
44. Content analysis (Pol)	H. Lasswell	1938–56	Chicago, Ill.
	I. deS. Pool		
	B. Berelson		
	P. Stone	1961–66	Cambridge, Mass.
45. Operant conditioning and learning; teaching machines (Psy)	B. F. Skinner	1938–58	Bloomington, Ind. Cambridge, Mass.
46. Statistical decision theory (Math)	A. Wald	1939–50	New York, N.Y.
47. Operations research and systems analysis (Math)	P. M. S. Blackett	1941–50	London, Eng.
	P. Morse	1941–58	Cambridge, Mass.
	R. Bellman		
48. Scaling theory (Psy)	L. Guttman	1941–54	Ithaca, N.Y.
	C. Coombs		Ann Arbor, Mich.

Type of support 5	No. of workers 6	Quantitative aspects 7	Years until impact 8
University chairs, research projects, and travel grants	3 + N	Non-Q	20 ± 10
University chairs	1	QPE	10 ± 5
Institute for social research and university	3 + N	QPI	20 ± 5
Government office	N	QFE	5
University and research institutes	1 + N	QPI	10 ± 5
Public research institutes and university chairs	1 + N	QFE	10 ± 5
University research institutes	4 + N	QPI	15 ± 5
University and research institutes, commercial organizations	3 + N	QFE	5
University chair	1 + N	QFE	15
University research institutes and government office	1 + N	QFE	10 ± 5
University institute	2	QFE	10
University chairs	1 + N	QPE	15
University chair	1 + N	QPE	15 ± 5
Government research institutes	N	QPE	5
University chairs	3 + N	QFE	10 ± 5

Contribution 1	Contributor 2	Time 3	Place 4
49. Quantitative models of nationalism and integration (Pol)	K. Deutsch B. Russett R. L. Merritt	1942–67	Cambridge, Mass. New Haven, Conn.
50. Theories of economic development (Ec)	P. Rosenstein-Rodan R. Prebisch R. Nurkse W. A. Lewis G. Myrdal A. O. Hirschman R. F. Harrod E. Domar H. Chenery	1943–58	London, Eng. Santiago, Chile New York, N.Y. Manchester, Eng. Stockholm, Swed. New Haven, Conn. Oxford, Eng. Baltimore, Md. Stanford, Calif.
51. Computers (Math)	V. Bush S. Caldwell D. P. Eckert J. W. Mauchly	1943–58	Cambridge, Mass. Philadelphia, Pa.
52. Multivariate analysis linked to social theory (Soc)	S. Stouffer T. W. Anderson P. Lazarsfeld	1944–54	Washington, D.C. Cambridge, Mass. New York, N.Y.
53. Information theory, cybernetics, and feedback systems (Math)	C. Shannon N. Wiener	1944–58	Cambridge, Mass. Orange, N.J.
54. Econometrics (Ec)	J. Tinbergen P. Samuelson E. Malinvaud	1935–40 1947 1964	The Hague, Neth. Cambridge, Mass. Paris, Fr.
55. Cognitive dynamics of science (Phil)	J. B. Conant I. B. Cohen T. Kuhn D. deS. Price	1946–64	Cambridge, Mass. Berkeley, Calif. New Haven, Conn.
56. Computer simulation of economic systems (Ec)	L. Klein G. Orcutt	1947–60	Philadelphia, Pa. Madison, Wis.
57. Structuralism in anthropology and social science (An)	C. Levi-Strauss	1949–66	Paris, Fr.
58. Hierarchical computerized decision models (Math)	H. Simon	1950–65	Pittsburgh, Pa.
59. Cost-benefit analysis (planned programming and budgeting) (Pol)	C. Hitch	1956–63	Santa Monica, Calif.
60. Computer simulation of social and political systems (Pol)	W. McPhee H. Simon A. Newell I. Pool R. Abelson	1956–66 1958–64	Pittsburgh, Pa. Cambridge, Mass. New Haven, Conn.
61. Conflict theory and variable sum games (Psy)	A. Rapoport	1960–	Ann Arbor, Mich.
62. Stochastic models of social processes (Math)	J. S. Coleman	1965	Baltimore, Md.

Type of support 5	No. of workers 6	Quantitative aspects 7	Years until impact 8
University chairs	1 + N	QFE	20 ± 5
Government offices, U.N. regional commission, university chairs	6 + N	QFE	10 ± 5
University and government research laboratories	N	QFE	10 ± 5
Government and university research institutes	3 + N	QFE	5
University research institute and Bell Laboratories	2 + N	QFE	10 ± 5
Government institute and university chairs	1 + N	QFE	10 ± 5
University chairs	3 + N	Non-Q	15
Research institutes	2 + N	QFE	5
Museum (government)	1 + N	QPI	15 ± 5
University research institute	1 + N	QPE	10
Government-related research institute	3 + N	QFE	7
University chairs and research institutes	2 + N	QPE	5 ± 3
University research institute	1 + N	QFE	2
University and research institute	1 + N	QFE	5

made their advance, particularly in physics and chemistry, in the years after World War I?

A third factor was fortuitous: the extraordinary transformation of universities in the U.S. after World War II. First there was the GI Bill which paid for college schooling of war veterans and brought millions of young men into the colleges and universities. Second was the demographic impact of the baby boom in the immediate postwar years which, following the ebbing of the first wave, produced a new tide of students for the schools. The expansion of the universities expanded the professoriate and the number of persons engaged in research.

The fourth factor brought all the others together: the fact that in the decades following World War II, the United States became the paramount power in the world and then found itself engaged in a Cold War with the Soviet Union for political dominance. A scientific rivalry, particularly in space exploration, intensified as the two countries competed for prestige. In mundane fact this meant that a huge research-and-development effort was now underwritten for the first time by the government and, in auxiliary instances, by the major foundations. The government needed foreign-area political, economic, and language specialists on the Soviet Union, China, Southeast Asia, Africa, the Middle East, Latin America, etc. The military needed not only weapons experts but individuals who could do systems analysis and operations research as well as the new kind of detailed logistical planning. The universities and businesses needed large numbers of specialists, particularly in such fields as economics, psychology, and political science, where the expansion was greatest.

Finally the rediscovery of social problems, particularly in the 1960s, focussed renewed attention on the social sciences. There were the problems of discrimination, poverty, broken families, poor housing environments, race riots, ecological and environmental problems, and the like. And the Kennedy and Johnson administrations responded with extraordinary rapidity in the adoption of social programs that required the "expert advice" of social science.

For all these reasons, the social sciences have been in the forefront of public attention and expectations in the past thirty or so years in a way that had never been true before in their history—short as it is.*

None of this would have been possible without the sense that a set of genuine intellectual advances had taken place in the social sciences which,

---

* The simplest way of establishing lineage is by patrilineal descent. In economics, the grandfathers—Adam Smith, Thomas Malthus, and David Ricardo, c. 1776–1810; the fathers—Alfred Marshall and Léon Walras, 1870–90. In sociology, the grandfathers—Auguste Comte, Karl Marx, and Herbert Spencer, c. 1850–70; the fathers—Émile Durkheim and Max Weber, 1890–1915. In psychology, the grandfathers—Hermann Helmholz, Ernst Weber, and Gustav Fechner, c. 1839–60; the fathers—Wilhelm Wundt, William James, and Sigmund Freud, 1879–1910. In anthropology, the grandfathers—Edward Burnett Tylor and James George Frazer, 1879–1900; the fathers—Franz Boas and Bronisław Malinowski, 1910–20. The dates are somewhat arbitrary, representing the period of major work and the establishment of reputation.

Table 2. Major Social Science Contributions by Field and Focus, 1900-65

Field	Total	Major contributions		Focus on theory		Focus on method		Focus on results	
	1900 to 1965	1900 to 1929	1930 to 1965	1900 to 1929	1930 to 1965	1900 to 1929	1930 to 1965	1900 to 1929	1930 to 1965
Psychology	13	7	6	6	3	6	6	6	6
Economics	12	5	7	4	5	4	6	5	7
Politics	11	7	4	7	2	2	4	4	4
Mathematical statistics	11	4	7	2	5	4	7	4	6
Sociology	7	6	1	4	1	5	1	6	1
Philosophy	5	3	2	3	2	2	2	0	1
Anthropology	3	1	2	1	2	0	2	1	2
Total	62	33	29	27	20	23	28	26	27

for the first time, were equipped to set forth theoretical and practical knowledge. While the source of many of these reorganizations or break-throughs of knowledge antedates the postwar period, the attention to the social sciences and the claims made by the social sciences were largely during the postwar period, and one is therefore justified in considering the period between 1945 and 1970 as a single period in which a set of promises were made—in disciplines, in methodology and techniques, and in social programs—which indicated that the social sciences had come of age. Given the fact, as we shall show, that many of these promises were not realized, it would be useful, even if only schematically as this must be, to review the major claims of the social sciences during this period.

Economics

In the postwar period, especially in the 1960s during the Kennedy adminis-tration, economists were regarded as individuals who had the "right an-swers" not only in managing the economy, but in the formulation of other social programs as well. The symbolic recognition of the status of economics came in 1969 when a Nobel Prize in Economics was established (the first prizes were awarded in 1901), and Ragnar Frisch of Norway and Jan Tinbergen of The Netherlands were jointly rewarded for their indepen-dent work in econometrics. The influence of economics has persisted in the Carter administration: of the fifteen cabinet-rank officials, four have Ph.D.'s in economics.*

---

* The four: W. Michael Blumenthal, Treasury; Juanita M. Kreps, Commerce; James R. Schlesinger, Energy: F. Ray Marshall, Labor. In addition, the Secretary of Defense, Harold Brown, has an academic degree and a Ph.D. in physics and was also president of the California Institute of Technology.

There were six areas in which economics forged ahead steadily during this period:

a) *The Keynesian revolution.* In a charming memoir about his economic upbringing and education, Paul Samuelson, who won the Nobel Prize in Economics in 1970, remarked: "The great romance in the life of any economist of my generation must necessarily have been the Keynesian revolution.... Economics itself was a sleeping princess waiting for the invigorating kiss of Maynard Keynes." And in a eulogy Samuelson wrote in 1946 on the death of Keynes, he remarked:

> ... It is quite impossible for modern students to realize the full effect of what has been advisably called "The Keynesian Revolution," upon those of us brought up in the orthodox tradition. What beginners today often regard as trite and obvious was to us puzzling, novel, and heretical....
>
> The *General Theory* caught most economists under the age of 35 with the unexpected virulence of a disease first attacking and decimating an isolated tribe of South Sea islanders. Economists beyond 50 turned out to be quite immune to the ailment. With time, most economists in-between began to run the fever, often without knowing or admitting their condition.[2]

The heart of Keynes's *Theory,* as it affected public policy, was the argument that a return to economic equilibrium (or a recovery from a depression) was not automatic in the capitalist economic system, even after a "wringing out" of "over-production," or a fall in the money-wage rate (which was difficult anyway), but could be managed by government intervention. There were two elements to the Keynesian diagnosis. One was that savings in the system did not automatically flow into investments, even if the interest rate was high. A second was that the level of economic activity, and hence of employment, depended on the level of aggregate demand. The heart of the Keynesian prescription, therefore, is what is called today "demand management." The mechanism is government fiscal policy, *i.e.,* the level of taxes and the degree of government spending.

b) *National income accounts.* The letters GNP and the term gross national product have passed so quickly into common usage that it is difficult to realize how recent was their adoption. In point of time, the collection of economic data to build a full set of national income accounts and to assess the gross national product was first proposed by Pres. Franklin D. Roosevelt in his budget message of 1945. Actually, the conceptual work and the empirical steps in this accounting were first done in the 1930s by Simon S. Kuznets (who won the Nobel Prize in 1971) in Pennsylvania and Colin Clark in Cambridge, England.

Gross national product is simply the sum total of the monetary value of all goods and services produced by a nation's economy during a single year. It consists, essentially, of two parts: one is the demand for goods and services at all stages of production—from raw materials to finished goods—as reflected in the prices of these goods and services; the other is the income, or the monies paid out to the individuals producing these goods and services. As final totals, the two sides match.

The national income accounts are like a set of building blocks of the economic system. They show what proportions of the total national product go for raw materials, domestic or imported, the cost of intermediate products and services, such as fabricating and finishing, and the totals of the final demands. Along the way, one can calculate the value added at each stage of the process. On the other side of the ledger, we can calculate the proportion of GNP going to individuals for personal consumption, the amounts taken by government and business corporations, and the like.

Each year's figures give us the *level* of economic activity; year-to-year figures allow us to measure the rate of growth, the rate of productivity, and the like. Since every major business corporation plans ahead to some extent —as to capital expansion, degree of inventory, amount of working capital, supply of labor, and the like—the forecasts of GNP clearly affect their plans and their judgments as to what decisions to make. For the government, the GNP is the basic tool to measure the level of employment, the unused capacity of the economy, and the expected degree of economic activity in order to set targets for growth, levels of unemployment, or inflation.

c) *Input-output analysis,* developed by Wassily Leontief (who won the Nobel Prize in 1973) is the physiology of the economic system—the interconnected transactions and flows between industries, and the effects of the shifts in the inputs or outputs of each industry on every other.

The input-output table—the idea in principle goes back to the *Tableau Économique* of the Physiocrats in late eighteenth-century France—is a rectangular grid, the heart of which is a square matrix of 81×81 rows and columns, providing a total of 6,561 cells which would be the "beehive" of the economy. Each row is an industry, and the table shows the interindustry transactions, the sales and purchases of each industry to the other, that tie together the highly differentiated system as a whole.

For purposes of analysis, the eighty-one industries are grouped into seven basic sectors, such as basic metal (*e.g.,* steel); basic nonmetal (*e.g.,* glass, paper, wood, plastic); energy (*e.g.,* oil, natural gas, coal); final metal (*e.g.,* automobiles, aircraft); final nonmetal (*e.g.,* shoes, clothing, furniture), and so on. There are, in addition, ten columns on the right which integrate these transactions into the GNP, such as personal consumption from each industry, investment, new construction, and so forth. Two rows at the bottom specify the imports in each row and the value added by the industry.

Within each cell are a number of input-output coefficients. Thus, one can tell at a glance the ratio of the dollar-flow input in each cell to the total output of the entire sector within which that industry is classified.

As one would imagine, the number of computations to chart these interindustry transactions, or the value added by each industry to a finished product, or the proportion of inputs of each cell to the sector whole, is staggering. When Leontief began this task in the late 1930s, it took about five years to complete the table for the economy, an effort which made the exercise primarily a tool for retrospective analysis. With the introduction of high-speed computers, the input-output table became a major tool for planning and analysis. Thus, with a complete table, one could quickly calculate what the effects would be of a five-fold increase in the price of oil on *all other* industries and sectors of the economy. In this way, the input-output table allows for an "isotope trace" of different measures, governmental and otherwise, on the "physiology" of the system as a whole.

d) *Mathematical analysis and econometric models.* Mathematical analysis is primarily an expression of *relations between variables* (*e.g.*, consumption and investment, wages and prices) in algebraic or some other mathematical notation. It does not necessarily involve numbers or amounts, *i.e.*, the magnitudes of these variables. The analyst is seeking a precise way to formulate these relationships and to manipulate them mathematically to see how they change under stipulated conditions. Econometrics begins with the statistical *aggregation of quantities, i.e.*, the sum totals of specific indices or variables, though when these aggregates are put into a model of the economy they are expressed as coefficients or magnitudes of these variables, and the model itself is then put into mathematical form.

Mathematics has a long history in economics. William Stanley Jevons, when he proposed the theory of marginal analysis, used calculus to measure the incremental changes in prices. Léon Walras, when he wrote his *Elements of Pure Economics* (1874), used mathematics to demonstrate his general economic equilibrium theory, *i.e.*, the way in which relative prices clear all markets simultaneously. But mathematics was usually regarded as a kind of shorthand, rather than as a way of expressing underlying structures or relations. Alfred Marshall, whose *Principles of Economics* (1890) codified the classical approach and informed all economic analysis until Keynes, insisted that mathematics was secondary and that all economic propositions should be put into literary form. For illustrative purposes, he used geometrical diagrams (*e.g.*, supply-and-demand curves, or product elasticities at different price levels), and he felt that these alone were sufficient.

Modern mathematical analysis begins with Paul Samuelson's *Foundations of Economic Analysis* (1947), originally his Ph.D. thesis in 1941; he argued that economics could only advance by putting literary expressions into mathematical propositions. Mathematics, Samuelson insisted, overcomes ambiguities which are inherent in literary expression and allows the economist to "manipulate" the variables more readily and with a greater degree of vigor. As Samuelson wrote in his memoir:

> . . . to a person of analytical ability, perceptive enough to realize that mathematical equipment was a powerful sword in economics, the world of economics was his oyster in 1935. The terrain was strewn with

beautiful theorems begging to be picked up and arranged in unified order. Only the other day I read about the accidental importation into South America of the African honey bee, with the resulting decimation of the local varieties. Precisely this happened in the field of theoretical economics: the people with analytical equipment came to dominate in every dimension of the vector the practitioners of literary economics.[3]

In his *Foundations*, for example, Samuelson established a formal mathematical model of the Keynesian "multiplier and accelerator" effects (*i.e.*, the "velocities" of income spent in consumption, or capital spent on investment) and, by choosing a variety of different "values" (*i.e.*, magnitudes) for the parameters (*i.e.*, the limiting variables) in the model, he was able to show the different scale of effects when individuals had different "propensities to consume" (*i.e.*, to spend and save different proportions of their incomes) or business firms made investments in different kinds of plants (*i.e.*, the extra acceleration of that spending).

An indicator of the spread of this mode of analysis is that while thirty years ago graduate students in economics did little or no mathematics, a graduate student today would not be admitted unless he or she were proficient in advanced algebra and calculus; and, while Samuelson's *Foundations* was difficult for his contemporaries, a graduate student is now expected to handle its mathematical reasoning with relative ease.*

Econometrics is the empirical application of economic theory through statistical inference and mathematical models. Statistical analysis in U.S. economics began principally with Wesley Clair Mitchell of Columbia University in the 1920s, through the National Bureau of Economic Research. A student of Thorstein Veblen, Mitchell was skeptical of orthodox economic theory, which seemed to be abstract and deductive, and he decided that one could only understand an economy by the empirical study of actual activities. He began by charting business cycles, and to do so he, along with such students of his as Arthur F. Burns, began to construct statistical indexes of different time-series (*e.g.*, retail sales, money supply, inventories) to see which were leading indicators of upswings and downswings and which were lagging indicators. Out of this pioneering work came the construction of aggregate indexes such as the consumer price index† and, from the work of Simon Kuznets, the national income accounts.

---

* I am indebted in this discussion to the essay on Paul Samuelson by William Breit and Roger Ransom in *The Academic Scribblers: American Economists in Collision* (New York: Holt, Rinehart & Winston, 1971).

† How can one lump together, say, apples and pears, clothing and automobiles? Because each can be expressed as a price per unit, and thus given a homogeneous form, one can weight the relative importance of the different purchases in a consumer's "market basket," and then aggregate these different prices and weights into a single index number. A single "normal" year is picked as the base, and the number for that year is called 100. Subsequent price changes are expressed in index number terms relative to that base year, so that a 10-percent increase in the cost of the items in that market basket makes the next year's numbers on the consumer price index 110.

A model is a representation of a reality. One can have a physical model, such as a small-scale model of an airplane, or the pictorial model of an atom, or a mathematical model, which translates relationships (*e.g.,* the price level, the interest rate, unemployment, and gross national product) into variables and writes mathematical equations for their relationships. The first U.S. economist to do model building was Lawrence Klein of the University of Pennsylvania Wharton School. In his first models, Klein used only twelve equations to represent the components of final demand, such as consumption, fixed investment, inventories, and the like. A contemporary model, such as that of Otto Eckstein of Harvard (the DRI model, from his Data Resources, Inc. company), has a total of 898 variables, most of which are expressed as ratios, square roots, and logarithms and are related through 800 equations.

The DRI model has 165 exogenous variables, which are factors outside the system, such as taxes, government outlays, and the like, and 733 endogenous variables, which are factors that relate to each other usually through market transactions. The DRI model, for example, has four broad sectors for fiscal policy, monetary policy, foreign sector, and supply. The fiscal policy variables correspond to the broad divisions of the national income accounts. The exogenous variables are government spending, foreign transfers, and the like. Endogenous spending variables are "transfer payments" (*e.g.,* social security) and the like. On the supply side, production is seen as the key determinant of investment and employment. The model uses an input-output matrix of seventy-five industries to produce a generated output series.

By running the 800 equations through a computer (using statistical aggregates on a quarterly basis), the econometric models seek to predict the major variables of economic activity for a year ahead and even for each quarter. These basic variables would be real gross national product, non-residential fixed investment, industrial production, consumer prices, wholesale prices, corporate profits, unemployment, and the like. The forecasts have become the basis of policy decisions by government, corporations, financial institutions, and the like.

e) *Growth models.* One should distinguish between theories of economic development and growth models. Theories of economic development are judgments about the most appropriate ways to spur economic development in a society and have been related directly to policy issues, particularly of the less developed nations. Growth models are an attempt to add a dynamic dimension to economic theory, which has been largely based on static considerations.

After World War II, many economists turned to the empirical question of how to spur economic development in a nation. The typical issues were: should one invest first in heavy industry (as the Soviet Union had done) or in agriculture? should one make heavy investment in human resources (*i.e.,* education) or bring in outside capital and skills? should there be balanced growth, between regions or economic sectors, or unbalanced growth, allowing any leading sector to develop even at the expense of others?

Much of the early writing concentrated on the role of planning and the adoption of government plans, and considerable ingenuity went into the development of these plans, as related by W. Arthur Lewis, one of the pioneers of the field, in his informative *The Theory of Economic Growth* (1955). But after a decade of work most of the theorizing in the field had diminished because of the realization that economic development was inextricably tied to political and social factors, and no satisfactory theory of these relationships had emerged.

Growth models, on the other hand, have sought to take neoclassical economic theory, which begins with fixed constants of capital and labor, and introduce a systematic theory of change. The major effort, whose pioneers have been Edward Denison and Robert M. Solow, has been to build a theory of technological change into the models of economic interactions.

f) *Welfare economics* is a field which has sought to define the optimal allocation of goods and services within equilibrium conditions. The famous theorem of Vilfredo Pareto, called "Pareto optimality," states that a distribution is optimal when at least one person is made better off, with no one being worse off. All other modes become *redistributive.* In game theory terms, this states that if one wins and another loses, it is a zero-sum game. However, if everybody wins, even in differential amounts, or no one loses, it is a nonzero-sum game. Much of the work in the field is highly theoretical. During the postwar years, there were two significant developments. One was the work of Kenneth J. Arrow, *Social Choice and Individual Values* (1951, originally his Ph.D. thesis, which, along with his work on equilibrium analysis, won him the Nobel Prize in Economics in 1972); the other was the book by John Rawls, *A Theory of Justice* (1971), which, though a work of political philosophy, drew much of its analysis of distributive justice from the welfare economics of the Indian economist Amartya K. Sen, now at Oxford University.

The Arrow volume establishes the fact that individuals can scale their preferences (*i.e.,* order their choices or buying decisions or voting preferences) in a rationally defensible way, but if certain conditions are observed, such as majority rule or transitivity (*i.e.,* if I prefer A to B, and B to C, logically I should prefer A to C), it is logically impossible to have a combined *social* choice (or, technically, a group welfare function) which assembles the discordant preferences of diverse individuals into a single, rationally ordered scale. The practical effect of Arrow's demonstration is to prove that theoretically there cannot be a single social choice that would satisfy or be approved by all the participants in a group or a society. What it means is that, if individuals are to work out discordant preferences peacefully, there will have to be bargaining and trade-offs, in which one group of individuals forgoes some preferences in order to achieve others.

Since many goods in the society are public goods, that is, not divisible into individual portions like private goods—a road is a public good, a weapons system is a public good—the problem of how to reach rational decisions in these matters becomes a vexing one. In this area, there has grown up a large literature under the rubric of "public choice," and individuals associated with these themes are such writers as Anthony Downs, James Buchanan, Gordon Tullock, Mancur Olson, and James Coleman.

If one reviews the promise of economics in this period, it added up to the belief that economists had learned how to manage (if not plan) an economy; that the business cycle was largely obsolete, since the government could flatten out the peaks and raise the troughs; that full employment was a possibility; that economic growth could be maintained; and that the "Keynesian revolution" had given economists the theoretical and practical tools to achieve all these goals.

Modeling the mind and society

The second great domain of promise for the social sciences in the post-World War II era came in the expectation that some new master sciences would arise which would allow the social sciences to understand the cognitive processes of the mind and to create control systems for the modeling and subsequent management of society. These ambitions are associated with a number of intellectual developments, principally *cybernetics, information theory, structural linguistics, artificial intelligence and automata theory,* and *general systems theory.* Since these developments weave in and out of each other, an effort to sort them out in some schematic form would miss the integrative hopes that underlie them—though there never was a single unified theory that sought to integrate these ideas in a formal discipline—so my presentation, necessarily, will be discursive.

Cybernetics is associated with the name of MIT mathematician Norbert Wiener, who in 1948 published a book entitled *Cybernetics: or Control and Communication in the Animal and the Machine.* Wiener thought he had coined the word from the Greek root *kybernētēs,* meaning a helmsman, or pilot, or a steersman of a vessel. Actually, the word occurs often in Plato, *kybernētikē,* as a subdivision of *technai,* as the art of steersmanship, and denotes for Plato the art of guiding men in society, *i.e.,* the art of government. In 1834 André-Marie Ampère, the eponymous source of our measure of electricity, wrote an ambitious *Essay on the Philosophy of the Sciences* and, in dealing with the management of government, he translated the Greek word into French as *cybernétique.* Ironically, Wiener's book first appeared in French, having been commissioned initially by a French publisher.

Wiener, who did not know of these antecedents, explained that his choice of the word was suggested by the precedent of James Watt in calling a mechanical regulator a "governor." Since he was dealing primarily with servomechanisms, *i.e.,* those that involved a feedback and readjustment to circumstances, Wiener used the term "steersman," or cybernetics.

The principle of cybernetics is suggested by the term. It is a set of control mechanisms to keep a machine or a system on its course, to allow for readjustments to the initial paths or to new paths where there have been deflections or obstacles, and to adapt the mechanism to the goals that have been set. Much of the theory went back to Wiener's practical experience in both world wars of establishing automatic gun controls, as in an anti-aircraft gun seeking to follow a plane taking a weaving or evasive course. The underlying elements are energy and information. The motor of the machine is operated by energy, but signals are given (information) which allow the machine to make the necessary corrections.

The heart of cybernetic theory is that of a "feedback loop," meaning information returned to the control source (by sensors or similar devices) and its readjustment mechanisms. The system is adaptive and homeostatic, having the tendency to maintain stability or equilibrium. More generally, it is a theory of communication and control. Cybernetics thus is not a single field but a theory which finds application in a number of diverse fields.

As the French writer George T. Guilbaud of l'École Pratique des Hautes Études in Paris, has put it:

> Cybernetics is not electronics, nor neurology, nor sociology; nor is it a theory peculiar to any of these fields. It simply borrows problems from these and other fields, hoping that the solution it discovers may have some useful applications. . . . The position of cybernetics is rather analogous to that of statistics, which finds its use in extremely diverse fields (psychology, sociology, astronomy, economics, biology, and so on) and derives its name from the one specialized application—the study of human societies or states—with which it has never lost contact despite its rise to independence.[4]

Information theory arose out of the work of Claude E. Shannon of MIT and Bell Laboratories. Its initial purpose was to design telephone switching circuits which would increase the channel capacity of the transmission system. But information theory quickly came to the algebra of logic, which is the algebra of choice, or the range of alternative possibilities in the routing of a message. The parlor game of "Twenty Questions" is often taken as a conventional illustration of how one narrows a range of possibilities by asking a yes or no question that divides a response into equally likely groups. As Shannon points out, in the article "Information Theory" that he wrote for the 14th edition of the *Encyclopædia Britannica:*

> The writing of English sentences can be thought of as a process of choice: choosing a first word from possible first words with various probabilities; then a second, with probabilities depending on the first; etc. This kind of statistical process is called a stochastic process, and

information sources are thought of, in information theory, as stochastic processes.

The information rate of written English can be translated into bits (binary digits of 1–0), and if each letter in the language occurred with equal frequency in a message, there would be 4.76 bits per letter. But since the frequencies are obviously disparate (E is highly common, for example, while Q and X are not), the actual rate is one bit per letter. Technically, English is said to be 80 percent "redundant," a fact that can be immediately ascertained by the ease of deciphering a sentence from which various vowels or consonants have been deleted. This is the basis of certain speed-writing courses, or the telegraphic transmissions of foreign correspondents, who save words and speed up transmission by compressing words (*e.g.*, compresng wrds) in their telegraphic copy.

By knowing the statistical structure of a language, one can derive a general formula which determines the rate at which information is produced by a stochastic process and, by proper encoding, create huge savings in transmission time. Transmission was the impetus to the formulation of information theory, but the core of the concept is the idea of coding, and the engine of the concept is the statistical theory which determines how a message should be encoded. Messages have to go through channels and inevitably become distorted by noise and other forms of distortion that arise from the physical property of the channel (*e.g.*, the copper telephone wire, or even optical fiber). What Shannon found was that it was possible to encode (*i.e.*, compress) a message so that it could be accurately transmitted even if the channel of communication was faulty, so long as there was enough capacity in the channel.

What is striking is how quickly the mathematical theory of communication took hold and spread into so many diverse fields. Randall L. Dahling, who has traced this process, points out:

> Dr. Shannon first set forth his theory in two articles which appeared in the *Bell System Technical Journal* in July and October of 1948. Here, he set down a unified theory of signal transmission based on the concept that transmitted information may be considered statistically and its probabilities figured. . . .
>
> The importance of the idea was instantly perceived. Other scientists started discussing it immediately, and, within a few months following its publication, new articles making use of the theory began to appear at an ever-increasing rate. At first, these new articles were restricted to communication engineering, but by November 1949, the theory had been applied to psychology (by F. C. Frick and G. A. Miller in the *Psychological Review*). Then in August 1950, H. Jacobson applied the theory in physiology and later extended it to optics (in *Science* on the informational capacity of the human ear, August 4, 1950; and on the informational capacity of the human eye, in *Science*, March 16, 1951). By November of 1950, the theory had established itself in physics (by

Dennis Gabor in *Phil. Mag.*), and in the same month it was carried to linguistics (by O. H. Strauss in the *Journal of the Acoustical Society of America*). In December of the same year, it was written about from biological and sociological viewpoints (by Nicholas Rashevsky in the *Bulletin of Mathematics and Biophysics*). By 1951, it was being discussed in statistical journals (by G. A. Barnard, in *J. Royal Statistical Society*) and still it continued to spread rapidly.[5]

Why the idea took hold so rapidly is fairly clear. The work was at the focal point of a number of intersecting needs, prompted by the demands of the military and of business in communication, automation, and computation. The theoretical and statistical underpinnings seemed to mesh with the more general theory of Wiener's *Cybernetics,* a work which, after its publication in English in 1948, went through seven printings in one year. What the work of Shannon and Wiener seemed to promise was the long-sought-for move toward a unified theory of physical and human behavior (at least in physiology, psychology, and linguistics) through the concept of information.

Linguistic theory is the third leg on which these new ambitions were rising, particularly in the work of Noam Chomsky at MIT. Chomsky's initial work was in structural linguistics, an effort to demonstrate that language, though the most widely dispersed of all human "artifacts" (*i.e.,* the existence of dozens of major streams of language, such as the Indo-European, Uralic-Altaic, Hamito-Semitic, Tai and Sino-Tibetan, and about 3,000 distinct languages, let alone dialects), has a basic syntactical structure (*i.e.,* word orders that control meaning) and that in every language there is a "deep structure" of a few rules which generate all other rules of grammar. While Chomsky began in structural linguistics, his work led him into fundamental issues in epistemology and psychology; one of the crucial debates in the postwar years was the argument between B. F. Skinner (and other behaviorists) and Chomsky on the way in which languages are acquired.

For Skinner, who is an empiricist, a child learns a language in associative building blocks, responding to stimuli, and having its efforts rewarded by response. Through conditioning, through reinforcement (*i.e.,* reward), and through stimulus generalization (*i.e.,* the widening of associations), a child learns a language.

For Chomsky, language acquisition is innate. As he has argued, a person's knowledge of a language is not "representable as a stored set of patterns, overlearned through constant repetition and detailed training, with innovation being at most a matter of 'analogy.' " Instead, "a person who knows a language has represented in his brain some very abstract system of underlying structures along with an abstract system of rules that determine, by free iteration, an infinite range of sound-meaning correspondence. Possession of this grammar is a fact which psychology and neurophysiology must ultimately account for."

For Chomsky, the "underlying deep structures [of syntax] vary slightly, at most, from language to language," and the structure of mind is such that a human being can, without knowing or having heard a large number of cases, grasp the rule which makes intelligible the structure of the language he or she is hearing, or speaking. As Chomsky argues:

> This is what one would expect . . . since it is difficult to imagine how operations of this type could be abstracted from data. There is certainly no process of generalization or association of any kind known to psychology or philosophy, or any procedure of analysis that is known in linguistics that can come close to determining structures of this kind. Again, it is to be expected that these operations and their general properties will be uniform across languages, and this seems to be the case.[6]

The combination of cybernetics, information theory, and Chomskyian linguistics had its most direct impact in the fields of cognitive psychology and in "artificial intelligence," or the theory and practice of logical automata, more popularly, if crudely, called "thinking machines." Ideally, it was hoped that information theory and linguistics would allow the psychologists to learn how the mind worked (and, as an analogue, to trace out these patterns in neurophysiological terms), enabling logicians and computer specialists to write programs that would allow the computer to become a general problem solver, rather than being just an incredibly fast idiot machine capable only of following detailed instructions.

Warren McCulloch, a neurophysiologist, sought to show that the central nervous system does have the kind of connectivity that cybernetic theory presupposed, and that the mind, when it "sees," does not simply reflect what is out there, as if the eye were a camera, but selects elements from perceptual experience to synthesize or cognize what it sees. As Stephen Toulmin, who has written an appreciation of both Wiener and McCulloch, has observed:

> The task of imagining how a machine might be devised that could match the mental performances of a man was a task of exact mathematical analysis, demanding formal ingenuity and precision of a positively baroque order. The task of seeing how the formal analysis of such mechanisms might then be used to throw light on the actual working of the human brain—in particular, upon its role in regulating human behavior—was one for clinical understanding, philosophical reflectiveness, and speculative imagination. At this point, the respective skills of Wiener the mathematician and McCulloch the psychiatrist and neurologist matched one another admirably. Norbert Wiener had the formal virtuosity to transform the mathematical analysis of the electronic control and communication systems developed during the Second World War into a general and abstract theory of self-correcting, quasi-intelligent mechanisms and interconnecting systems. The idea of "negative feedback"—already implicit in the original design for the steam-engine governor and used by Claude

Bernard in the 1860's as a crucial element in a new style of physiological explanation—could thus be extended to yield a general account of self-controlling, or cybernetic, mechanisms. Meanwhile, all Warren McCulloch's empirical familiarity with the actual relations between brain and behavior—ranging from neuroanatomical studies on the structure and interconnections of the cerebral cortex in the higher apes to the accumulated clinical experience of human neurological disorders during his years as a psychiatrist—put him in a special position to judge how these new styles of mathematical and physiological analysis could be used to unravel the actual neurophysiological interactions within the brain.[7]

The major effort to combine information theory with cognitive psychology was made by George A. Miller of Harvard (now at Rockefeller University). In a classic article, seductively entitled "The Magical Number Seven, Plus or Minus Two," Miller suggests that there may be an intrinsic reason why the number seven is so appealing to us. Apart from the whimsy, Miller points out that on single-dimension stimuli (*e.g.*, pitch, loudness, points on a line), the span of absolute judgment that individuals possess in the number of discriminations they can make, or the amount of information that one can transmit, or the span of immediate memory, is about seven distinguishable alternatives—a rather small and limiting number for information processing. As Miller writes:

There seems to be some limitation built into us either by learning or by the design of our nervous systems, a limit that keeps our channel capacities in this general range. On the basis of the present evidence it seems safe to say that we possess a finite and rather small capacity for making such unidimensional judgments and that this capacity does not vary a great deal from one sensory attribute to another. . . .

There is a clear and definite limit to the accuracy with which we can identify absolutely the magnitude of a unidimensional stimulus variable. I would propose to call this limit *the span of absolute judgment,* and I maintain that for unidimensional judgments this span is usually somewhere in the neighborhood of seven.

Yet, in daily life we can identify accurately any one of several hundred faces, or any one of several thousand words, and the question is how are we able to overcome these limitations of perceptual and discriminatory capacities. What happens, says Miller, is that human beings have the capacity for recoding, or the ability to "embed" the bits of information they receive into larger and larger chunks. A man beginning to learn a telegraph code hears each dot and dash as a separate chunk, but then the sounds become recognized as letters—parts of larger chunks of words.

Miller, one of the most graceful writers in psychology, began his essay with the fascinating question why the history of human culture seems to have been so preoccupied with the "magical" number seven—the seven wonders of the world, the seven seas, the seven levels of hell, the seven days of the week, the win-or-lose of point seven in gambling dice—and though it may be only metaphoric to suggest some innate limit on our capacity to discriminate or to hold in our heads no more than seven distinctions (plus or minus two, as the statistical variance of the span), the more useful finding, which Miller derived from information theory, was not only the breakdown of information into bits as a way of measuring perceptual and discriminatory abilities, but the phenomenon of "recoding." For, as Miller points out:

> . . . recoding is an extremely powerful weapon for increasing the amount of information we can deal with. In one form or another we use recoding constantly in our daily behavior. . . . Our language is tremendously useful for repackaging material into a few chunks rich in information . . . the kind of linguistic recoding that people do seems to me to be the very lifeblood of the thought processes.[8]

Miller has also tried to show that the writing of computer programs illuminates the way individuals think. In computer programs, main routine operations are often interrupted to perform subroutines (additional side problems, such as incidental computations, in order to proceed with the main problem); and programs that allow this are called "recursive." A nonrecursive program is one where the computer does not return to the original routines, or other subroutines, and this process of failing re-entry is likely to clobber the machine's memory. Miller points out that individuals use subroutines in their own cognitive operations, both recursive and non-recursive, and the question is which do they use and how?

> One way to investigate this question presents itself in the realm of language. It is a feature of natural language—by "natural language" I mean the languages we ordinarily use in speaking to one another, as opposed to the "artificial languages" that we have developed for mathematics, logic, computer programming, and so on—that sentences can be inserted inside of sentences. For example, "The king who said, 'My kingdom for a horse,' is dead" contains the sentence, "My kingdom for a horse" embedded in the middle of another sentence, "The king is dead."
>
> Think of a listener as processing information in order to understand this sentence. Obviously, his analysis of one sentence must be interrupted while he analyzes the embedded sentence. When he finishes analyzing the embedded sentence, he must then resume his analysis of the original sentence. Here we have all the elements present in a computer subroutine.

Miller notes that even though such sentences are grammatical, they are difficult to follow or understand, and this suggests that our ability to use subroutines which refer to themselves must be rather limited.* But the intention in comparing cognitive operations with computer programs is to show that "often very general principles . . . govern the operation of any device, living or nonliving, capable of performing the operation in question. It is not a matter of reducing men to machines, but of discovering general principles applicable to men and machines alike. And this is the exciting prospect that I wish to display for your consideration."[9]

The idea of "artificial intelligence" was stimulated by the British mathematician Alan Mathison Turing, who during World War II was the principal designer of the "Ultra" machine which broke the German transmission codes. He raised the question whether a computing machine can think, or, to avoid the anthropomorphism inherent in such a statement, whether machines can be programmed to behave in the way we behave when we say we are thinking. John von Neumann, the great mathematician who was responsible for some of the major developments in electronic computers, went further and, in his paper, "The General and Logical Theory of Automata" (1951), laid down the conditions whereby automata, using digital (all-or-none) or analogical procedures, could engage in reasoning similar to formal logic and the means whereby automata could produce automata, or become, in effect, self-reproducing machines.

Von Neumann's program was very broad, but in the 1950s and 1960s a sustained effort was made, principally by Marvin Minsky and his associates at MIT, to write computer programs that would "reason," *i.e.,* prove mathematical theorems, untangle linguistic difficulties, and solve problems. The crucial step in the development of artificial intelligence was breaking away from the idea that a computer could solve a problem only when every single step in the procedures—and therefore the solution—is clearly specified by the programmer. On that basis, of course, a computer is simply a rapid tool for human use, and no more. What artificial-intelligence programmers proposed to do was to write a set of general rules into the program which would allow the computer to make analogies, or to follow steps of formal logic, or to analyze and break down complicated statements for purposes of computation, and to employ "heuristics" in the instructions to the computer. A computer is ruled by an algorithm which is an instruction for procedure, or a decision rule. In the most mechanical algorithm, a computer might go through every cell in a memory, or make every permutation

---

* To illustrate the difficulty of these recursive sentence-clauses, Miller begins generating a nest within a nest within a nest:

The question, of course, is whether we can do this more than once, that is to say, recursively. Let us try: *"The person who cited, 'The King who said, "My kingdom for a horse" is dead,' as an example is a psychologist."* Most people find that just on the borderline of intelligibility: if I had not prepared you for it, you probably would not have understood. Let us go one step more: *"The audience who just heard, 'The person who cited, "The king who said, 'My kingdom for a horse,' is dead,"' as an example is a psychologist,' is very patient."* By now you should be ready to give up. If not, of course, I could go on this way indefinitely.

and combination possible, in order to pick out the correct answer. But for some problems, this would take considerable time, even for a high-speed computer. Heuristics simply means a command to make probable judgments based on comparisons of likeness or similarity, or some similar rule which would make a search procedure more rapid. It is, in effect, a procedure for skipping, or jumping about, the way a mind grasps for clues, in order to combine the relevant steps for coming to a solution.

This is the basis of the checkers, and now the chess, programs that are stored in computers. But it also underlies the effort to have the computer "read" verbal statements of a problem and translate these into mathematical terms. Minsky gives an example of a program called "Student," created by Daniel Bobrow at MIT.

> The remarkable thing about Student is not so much that it
> understands English as that it shows a basic capacity for understanding
> anything at all. When it runs into difficulty, it asks usually pertinent
> questions. Sometimes it has to ask the person operating the computer,
> but often it resolves the difficulty by referring to the knowledge in its
> files. When, for instance, it meets a statement such as "Mary is twice as
> old as Ann was when Mary was as old as Ann is now," the program
> knows how to make the meaning of "was when" more precise by
> rewriting the statement as two simple sentences: "Mary is twice as old
> as Ann was X years ago. X years ago Mary was as old as Ann is now."[10]

The promise of artificial intelligence is not as bright today as it seemed fifteen or twenty years ago, when the enthusiasm was first kindled. Yet, it is always difficult to quell the flame of true believers; nor can one, should one, rule out a field by fiat because its initial claims may not have been realized. It is a question we shall return to in a later section.

Holistic visions

In anthropology and sociology, three movements dominated the field in the quarter century after the war.

In anthropology, there was the new interdisciplinary study called "culture and personality." One can go back to Ruth Benedict's *Patterns of Culture* (1934) for the seminal idea of this. Each culture, Benedict sought to demonstrate, has a basic configuration, and one can describe cultures in terms of their integrative principles. The idea was drawn, specifically, from Oswald Spengler's *Decline of the West* (1926–28), in which Western culture was called Faustian, and Arabic culture Magian. It was similar to Pitirim Sorokin's argument, in *Social and Cultural Dynamics* (4 vol., 1937–41), that cultural mentalities could be divided into the "ideational" and the "sensate" and that history was an alternation between these two ideal types. Essential to all these holistic conceptions was the idea that a single thread ran through all dimensions of a culture, so that the Faustian, or the sensate, elements impregnated all aspects of life, from science through the arts, values, and life-styles. In principle, it was an extension of Marx's belief that the dominant mode of production suffused all other aspects of a society so that, as in capitalism, where workers were treated as commodities—as objects for sale—all other elements, including art, became commodities as well.

While Marx, Spengler, and Sorokin painted their strokes on a broad historical canvas over long periods of time, Benedict sought to apply the idea of "integration" to individual cultures, seeing in each some single principle which defined them through some dominant cultural pattern. Her two modal types were Apollonian and Dionysian, terms she took from Friedrich Nietzsche's *Birth of Tragedy* (1872) to describe two fundamental views of the world. For her, the Pueblo Indians of the North American Southwest were Apollonian because of their harmonious way of life, whereas the Kwakiutl peoples of the Pacific Northwest were Dionysian in the fever pitch of frenzy and ecstasy that marked their rituals. A third culture, the Dobu, were repressed, hostile, inimical to one another; Benedict gave them no metaphorical designation, though at one point she compared their temperament with that of the early American Puritans.

The idea that there were discernible cultural patterns quickly led to the idea that these had to be embodied in the personality attributes of the individuals composing the culture. Especially after World War II, a large number of anthropologists and psychologists—Lloyd Warner, Alfred I. Hallowell, Melford Spiro, and others—began studying cultures in these terms. In some situations, such as the cooperative work of the anthropologist Cora Du Bois and the psychoanalyst Abram Kardiner with the people of Alor, Kardiner analyzed "blind" a set of projective tests (Rorschach, Thematic Apperception) and anthropological field protocols to make various judgments on the culture which were matched, independently, by Du Bois's description of the people.

The idea of "culture and personality" merged, quickly, into the study of "national character." The theme was put forth that individuals in a nation exhibited certain unitary patterns which were also embodied in the modal personality traits of its people. Benedict did a study of the Japanese, *The Chrysanthemum and the Sword* (1946); Erich Fromm did an analysis of the "anal-sadistic" features of German character, which predisposed the German people to authoritarianism, in his book *Escape from Freedom* (1941); Theodor W. Adorno, drawing on unpublished work of the Frankfurt Institute of Social Research, *Authority and the Family*, wrote *The Authoritarian Personality* (1950) with Nevitt Sanford and Elsie Frenkel-Brunswick, two psychologists, seeking to uncover the latent dispositions to Fascism in American society; the anthropologists Margaret Mead and Geoffrey Gorer did studies of the Russian character in which they argued that early patterns of infant swaddling led to a character that was extreme in its explosiveness and repression; Henry Dicks, a British psychiatrist, and Nathan Leites, a political scientist, psychoanalytically trained, sought to identify the salient characteristics of Bolshevik personality. For more than two decades, anthropology, personality theory, and to some extent sociology were dominated almost entirely by the field of "culture and personality." Yet by the 1970s, the field had all but completely disappeared. Why this happened is a fascinating intellectual puzzle, and we shall return to it in the next section.

The second promise was in sociology, where a similar "functionalist" emphasis (but deriving more directly from the work of Émile Durkheim, and indirectly from the functionalism of Bronisław Malinowski) dominated the field until the early 1970s. The leading figure, and a powerful theorist, was Talcott Parsons of Harvard. For Parsons, a society was integrated through its "value system" and these values, expressed as norms governing behavior, or prescribing the roles individuals played, legitimated the basic modes of conduct in society. Thus, American society would be characterized as valuing instrumental activism and achievement—elements drawn from the Protestant heritage with its this-worldly orientation (as against quietism, or pietism, or the otherworldly orientations of Buddhist and non-Western societies) and its Calvinist injunction to strive and work. In the work of Robert K. Merton of Columbia, these ideas were applied to the ways in which different "roles" were patterned in the social structure.

But Parsons had a far greater ambition: to create a general theory of social action. In this respect, Parsons went farther than any sociologist of his time and, in so doing, revealed the limits, and weakness, of that approach.

To write a general theory, one must be able to define the complete range of types of action (technically, to close a system), so that one can make deductive statements about the kinds of action (*e.g.*, a revolution) and the conditions under which they might occur. It is a model drawn from science, in particular from classical mechanics. To do this, Parsons had to achieve two theoretical goals.

The first was to define a set of terms that could give one an exhaustive range of possible combinations of action (in the sense that Newtonian mechanics provides the least number of laws from which one can deduce all possible future states of the celestial system). Sociology, up to the turn of the twentieth century, was cast largely in historical terms, *e.g.*, Marx's notion of social evolution of the modes of production from slavery to feudalism to capitalism. But Marx assumed a determinate pattern to this evolution in which socialism was the natural successor to capitalism. This assumed, first, that the Western pattern (based either on the development of rationality, or Hegel's ideas of consciousness, or man's technical mastery of nature and economic production) was the mode all other civilizations would follow, and second, that the *marche générale* of history was more or less inexorable.

If such a determinism did not exist, then one was left, as with Wilhelm Dilthey, in the swamp of historical relativism.

The first generation of sociologists (*i.e.*, Ferdinand Tönnies, Émile Durkheim, and Max Weber) sought to escape from this deterministic philosophy of history, or inconclusive relativism, by seeking to define some modal, ahistorical types of social relationships, such as *Gemeinschaft* and *Gesellschaft*, or organic and mechanical solidarity, or traditional and rational actions, by which social patterns could be classified. The basic contrast was between close-knit, face-to-face, primordial and undifferentiated groups (kin or tribe or small neighborhoods) and the impersonal, associational, differentiated type of urban society.

For Parsons this typology was too simple, and he sought to substitute for it what he called (in *The Social System*, 1951) the basic "pattern variables,":

Norms: universalistic or particularistic
Statuses: achieved or ascribed
Obligations: specific or diffuse
Emotions: neutral or affective

Norms are universalistic when a merit system open to all is used, while criteria are particularistic when some groups are singled out for more favorable treatment than others, *e.g.*, affirmative action. Statuses or positions are either achieved on the basis of individual ability, or ascribed, either because of birth, as in hereditary systems, or through assignment, as where quotas apply. In a similar way, societies may be seen as predominantly of one kind or mixtures in the way they employ these different values. The United States and Britain, for example, may differ because of the way in which social mobility in the United States is more open (universalistic) and that of Britain more circumscribed (particularistic). The point of this scheme is that one has an exhaustive vocabulary for dealing with all kinds of social situations and types of societies.

Parsons went even further, in that (together with Edward A. Shils and the collaboration of Harvard colleagues, such as the anthropologist Clyde Kluckhohn and the psychologist Gordon W. Allport) he sought to write a general theory of action which would have the effect of constructing an all-embracing system for the analysis of social actions, in the way Léon Walras had constructed a general equilibrium theory for economics. One crucial consideration that governs this intention has to be understood. A general theory is not a descriptive set of statements, or a summary of empirical knowledge about action. It is an analytical framework which would allow the social scientist a way of sorting out different kinds of action, of understanding the levels of complexity, and of making relevant comparisons of seemingly disparate phenomena. The model again is classical mechanics. But in the logic of that mode, the scientist does not deal with concrete bodies, but with aspects, or properties, of *all* bodies taken as a single whole. Thus Galileo, in dealing with the law of falling bodies, did not, could not, describe the trajectory of a *single* body (it is subject to too many contingent vicissitudes) but described the properties of *any* body during a fall, such as mass, acceleration, velocity, etc. In the same way, a general theory does not deal with concrete societies but with society as an analytical abstraction and with the properties of society as analytical dimensions. In the Parsons scheme, there is a cultural system (having four dimensions — cognitive, expressive, evaluative, and transcendental), a social system with four dimensions, a personality system, and an organism system. One could say, for example, that the four dimensions of the cultural system could just as easily be denoted as science, art, philosophy, and religion. But to do so would be to treat these as independent entities, whereas Parsons is interested in seeing the way in which they are attributes of a single cultural system.

In a similar way, Parsons endeavored to show how any social unit sought to maintain its stability, or equilibrium, by fulfilling four functions — of goal definition, integration, adaptiveness, and management of tensions — and that the different institutions of society — the economy, government, cultural institutions — had become specialized in undertaking one or another of these functions.

Before any criticisms are leveled — and many of these are trivial ones or of a know-nothing sort, using the epithet "jargon," a term which would not be applied, for example, to the technical vocabulary of poetic analysis — the intentions have to be understood. Marx had sought to write a general theory of society using such terms as "substructure and superstructure," "mode of production," "class struggle," and the like. Marx assumed that the secret of society lay in the underlying class divisions as rooted in the structure of production, and he had few ways of accounting for the autonomy or variation of political and cultural systems. (Thus Imperial Germany, the Weimar Republic, Nazi Germany, and the postwar Federal Republic were all, in their economic mode, capitalist, yet the political structures were highly variant.) Max Weber sought to provide an analytical framework by dealing primarily with the types of rational and nonrational action in society. Parsons went furthest in the logic of an *ahistorical* analysis by seeking to write a complete morphology of society. The enormous effort, over a thirty-five-year period, is one of his huge contributions to social science.

There is a sense, however, in which the effort may have been a failure. The reason may lie less in the level of abstraction than in the recalcitrance of sociology to the model which guided Parsons's effort, that of classical mechanics. Economics, for example, does not deal with concrete items — such as steel, tin, or rubber — other than translating these into abstract categories such as "production function" (the varied mix of capital and labor at relative prices) or "propensities to consume," and further making them homogeneous and linear by converting these into a single metric — money — and still further manipulating the exchange ratios in theoretical analysis. Such terms as investment, prices, or consumption apply to all societies, but equally one can see how these are exchanged to form an interconnected system. Sociology has terms that are general, such as power, authority, and status, but it is difficult to put these into metrics of exchange, and one can create only formal typologies, such as Montesquieu's classification of aristocracy, republics and monarchies, or contemporary usages of democracy—authoritarian, totalitarian, and the like. In short, a general theory, even if it creates a successful vocabulary that allows us to see the full range of human action, lacks a means of actually showing the processes of exchange, and, even assuming that societies or institutions seek to maintain an equilibrium or homeostatic balance, the means of analyzing these processes are perhaps only metaphorical.

Structural-functionalist sociology has been charged (*see* Alvin Gouldner's *The Coming Crisis of Western Sociology*, 1970) with being politically conservative because of its focus on integration and equilibrium. But problems of structural-functionalist analysis, au fond, are really epistemological and philosophical. They lie at the heart of the issue whether a social science, particularly sociology, can ever have a general theory of society or create a closed system. Marx sought to create a general theory, which was functionalist in its way, since he assumed that every society hangs together by some inner principle, which for him was the mode of production. Parsons took the same logic to its limit by seeking to create a comprehensive morphology of social institutions and social actions. The effort was an honorable one. More, it is one of the great intellectual feats of that generation. But the failure, perhaps, to fulfill the promise does not indicate a lack of greatness; it shows that the reach may be, necessarily, greater than the grasp.

A third major promise was evident in the social sciences, particularly in the 1960s. This was the effort to use social science for social-policy purposes. Since the efforts were so diverse, and many of them were simply empirical—*i.e.*, involved the use of techniques for purposes of investigation and analysis without relating these to any body of theory—it would be difficult to compile an inventory of these efforts, even the significant inquiries. I can briefly indicate the intentions and nature of these movements.

a) *Social indicators*. The example of the economists, in setting up, after World War II, a system of macroeconomic accounts, inevitably turned the attention of the sociologists to the question whether a similar system of social indicators could be created, and even whether these indicators could be integrated into a set of social accounts similar to the national economic accounts. Thus, for example, the question was posed: we know how much money is being spent for doctors, nurses, and hospitals, but is the country "healthier" or not? Or, we know how much money is spent for schools and teachers, but do students know more? Or, we have had large-scale migrations from farms to cities, and vast regional shifts around the country; are such migrations disrupting families? is there a relation between migration rates and crime, and so forth? In 1966 the U.S. Department of Health, Education, and Welfare set up a panel on social indicators headed by Daniel Bell and William Gorham, who was later succeeded by Alice Rivlin, with Mancur Olson as staff director. A document by that panel, entitled "Toward a Social Report," was published in 1966, in the closing days of the Johnson administration. Since then there have been many efforts to develop social indicators of different kinds for environmental adequacy, quality of life, and the like. For various reasons—and these are discussed in the next section—the results have been mixed and the promises largely unfulfilled.

b) *Social forecasting.* In 1965 the American Academy of Arts and Sciences set up a Commission on the Year 2000 chaired by Daniel Bell. It had thirty members, including Wassily Leontief, Zbigniew Brzezinski, Daniel P. Moynihan, Robert C. Wood, and other individuals who went on to government service in various positions. After two book publications, *Towards the Year 2000* (1968), edited by Bell, and *The Year 2000* (1967), edited by Herman Kahn and Anthony Wiener, which was sponsored by the Commission, ten work groups were set up to explore various issues, from the structure of the U.S. government (resulting in a book edited by Harvey S. Perloff, *The Future of the United States Government Toward the Year 2000,* 1971) to questions of values and rights, the life-cycle, the future of computers, cultural institutions, and the like.

The "Futurist" movement spread rapidly and widely.* Parallel movements began in England, France, and Poland. Large numbers of organizations have devoted themselves to systematic forecasting. The World Future Society, an organization of 25,000 members, has become a clearing house for various studies and speculations. Again, the results have fallen far short of the promises, a question to be discussed in the next section.

c) *Social evaluation.* Today social evaluation has become an established feature of government policy. When billions of dollars are spent for government programs, it is inevitable that the government will also want to know how well the programs are working and to what extent policy can be guided by research results.

The foremost example of social evaluation—and the one that has received the most attention for a decade—is the so-called "Coleman Report," by James S. Coleman, then at Johns Hopkins University and now at the University of Chicago, on the effect of segregated school environments on the achievement levels of minority pupils in the elementary and high schools of the country.

The Civil Rights Act of 1964 contained a section, virtually unnoticed, which instructed the Commissioner of Education to conduct a survey on "the lack of availability of equal educational opportunities," by reason of race, religion or national origin. Over a two-year period, Coleman and his associates tested nearly 600,000 children (in five different grades) in 4,000 schools in all 50 states and the District of Columbia, while questioning 60,000 teachers and the principals in these schools as well. The 737 page report, *Equality of Educational Opportunity,* was published by the U.S. Government Printing Office in 1966.

The report made two points: minority children have a serious educational deficiency at the start of school, in grade one, which is obviously not a

---

* *See* "The Planning of the Future," by Bertrand de Jouvenel in *The Great Ideas Today, 1974.*

result of school; and they have an even more serious deficiency at the end of school, in grade twelve, which is obviously in part a result of the school. What made this startling, and quite grave, was the premise which Coleman (and implicitly a liberal society) had: namely, that schools are successful only insofar as they reduce the dependence of a child's opportunities upon his social origins. The effectiveness of schooling was to be measured by its ability to overcome the differences in the starting point of children from different social groups, and the schools were not doing this.

In proof of these conclusions, Coleman pointed out—by the matching of different schools, and by the multivariate analysis of different factors—that such elements as per pupil expenditure, books in the library, and a host of similar facilities and curricular measures had virtually no relation to achievement if the "social" environment of the school, *i.e.,* the educational backgrounds of other students and teachers, is held constant. This led Coleman to argue that *"the sources of inequality of educational opportunity appear to lie first in the home itself and the cultural influences immediately surrounding the home; then they lie in the schools' ineffectiveness to free achievement from the impact of the home, and in the schools' cultural homogeneity which perpetuates the social influences of the home and its environs."*[11]

The curious fact is that at first the Coleman Report went virtually unnoticed. There was no story in the *New York Times* or other national media. The first discussion appeared in the public policy quarterly *The Public Interest* and was soon followed in various educational magazines and then, quickly, in the foundations and the black community itself. One crucial element of the report was singled out for special attention—the discussion of the cultural homogeneity of the schools. And the response, particularly of the black community, was: if this is the case, then de facto segregation of schools (which are a product of residential, not legal, segregation) had to be ended; and the principal means would have to be the busing of black children to white schools and vice versa.

Busing became one of the most vitriolic and divisive issues in community political life. Entire cities, such as Boston, Detroit, and Los Angeles, were torn apart by the issue. Little or no attention was paid to Coleman's other major point, the problem of the initial home environments of minority children, a question that had been raised in 1965 by the "Moynihan Report" on the black family, when Moynihan was assistant secretary of labor in the Johnson administration, nor to the fact that busing alone might not be sufficient. As Coleman wrote in an article in *The Public Interest:*

> It is not a solution simply to pour money into improvement of the physical plants, books, teaching aids, of schools attended by educationally disadvantaged children. For other reasons, it will not suffice merely to bus children or otherwise achieve pro forma integration. (One incidental effect of this would be to increase the segregation within schools, through an increase in tracking.)

The only kinds of policies that appear in any way viable are those which do not seek to improve the education of Negroes and other educationally disadvantaged at the expense of those who are educationally advantaged. This implies new kinds of educational institutions, with a vast increase in expenditures for education—not merely for the disadvantaged, but for all children. The solutions might be in the form of educational parks, or in the form of private schools paid by tuition grants (with Federal regulations to insure racial heterogeneity), public (or publicly-subsidized) boarding schools (like the North Carolina Advancement School), or still other innovations.[12]

One can leave aside the viability of these specific proposals. The point is that Coleman, as a sociologist, approached the problem in terms of the complete social environment of the disadvantaged child—family, home, and school. But the report became the focus of a political division on one issue alone—that of busing. The Coleman Report was probably the most massive social science report in American society in the last several decades. Its findings and its fate are instructive.

Difficulties and disappointments

If one reviews the major theoretical advances in the social sciences from 1940 to 1970, almost all of them have been qualified to some extent, substantially or otherwise.

In economics, Keynesian theory has come increasingly under attack. One reason has been its neglect of monetary theory. To the neoclassical economists of Alfred Marshall's time, the level of economic activity was measured, and to some extent controlled, by monetary measures and monetary policy. To the Keynesians, or at least to the extremists among them, money did not matter. Since they saw, in the depression years, a weak link between the changes in the stock of money and the level of aggregate demand, they argued that monetary policy had little or no impact on the level of economic activity. In the last decade this argument has been hotly challenged by Milton Friedman and his followers. A second factor has been the argument that "macroeconomic" policy is too clumsy a means of managing, or as the saying goes, "fine-tuning," an economy. Thus, economists returned to "microeconomics," or the behavior of individuals and firms, and are seeking, through the analysis of the *expectations* of these units, to understand the relationship between micro- and macro- activity. A third argument is that Keynesian economics, by concentrating largely on effective demand, assumed that supply would simply be a response to changes in demand; yet the argument is now made that changes in supply (*e.g.,* investment in new energy sources, or substitutions of limited metals or minerals) is more a function of government policy, or of long-run expectations, and that Keynesian theory has not been equipped to deal with these questions.

The crucial problem has been the intractability of inflation. Keynesian economics had won its spurs by being able to suggest measures to aid recovery from recession. President Kennedy's tax cut in the 1962 budget, suggested by Walter Heller, was taken as proof of the efficacy of Keynesian measures. Yet Keynesian theory, seemingly, has been unable to account for inflation, and this has given rise to the monetarist counterattack. We shall return to this question in the second part of this article on new directions in the social sciences.

The use of GNP measures to assess economic growth has been questioned, for reasons that are quickly apparent in the nature of the measuring instruments. For one thing, GNP is a measure of transactions *in the market* and necessarily cannot take into account services in the household (*e.g.,* the work of the wife) or consumption on a farm, which may enhance a family's well-being but which is not registered in the market. (As Arthur C. Pigou, the successor to Marshall at Cambridge and one of the founders of modern welfare economics, once remarked: "If a widowed vicar has a housekeeper, and pays her a wage, that is an addition to the national income. If the vicar then marries the housekeeper, it is a subtraction from the national income.") The second reason is that GNP is simply an *addition* of all goods and services and makes no distinction among them. Thus, if a plant spills wastes in a river, which then has to be cleaned up, the subsequent costs of reducing pollution become an addition to GNP. In recent years economists such as James Tobin of Yale University have sought to create a modified GNP by making such subtractions which presumably do not actually increase the quality of life by an index of net national welfare. But the conceptual difficulties of defining quality and welfare have been quite great.

Econometric models have become more complicated and are employed more widely than ever before, but the problem of accuracy of forecasts bedevils the model makers. There are two reasons for this: one is that the important variables are exogenous, *i.e.,* stand outside the system, such as political decisions, and these are difficult to account for; two, the rising degrees of uncertainty (as people seek different ways to defend themselves against inflation) introduce perturbations in the economy, and the models cannot easily follow these at times wildly fluctuating effects. (I shall expand on this somewhat, in the concluding paragraphs of this section, which deal with some of the theoretical limits of the social sciences.)

While modeling the economy has proved recalcitrant, modeling the mind has been even more so. If there is a single term that can sum up the problem, it is "complexity." The number of cells in the human body is somewhere on the general order of 10^{15} or 10^{16}. The number of neurons in the central nervous system is somewhere on the order of 10^{10}. As John von Neumann remarked: "We have absolutely no past experience with systems of this degree of complexity." Whether we can master such complexity is moot. Language, too, has presented some unforeseen hurdles. When linguists began to discover basic *syntactical* rules of word order, mathematicians and computer scientists thought it would be a comparatively simple matter to do machine translation, whereby computers would be able, automatically, to translate one language into another. But natural languages, while following syntactical rules that can be duplicated by constructed or machine languages, present *semantic* difficulties (meaning, nuance, ambiguity, inflection) that are not easily assimilated from one language to another. Idiom alone can be defeating. The popular story is that the phrase "out of sight, out of mind" was translated into Chinese and then translated back literally as "invisible idiot." While a phrasebook of idioms might be programmed into a computer, the larger problems of ambiguity and nuance are not so easily solved, and, except for some simple and highly denotative language sets, or some highly specialized scientific terminology, the idea of machine translation has been all but completely abandoned by linguists today.

If complexity has been the stone of stumbling in the cognitive fields, simplicity has been the undoing of some of the sociological theories. One reason why the large field of "culture and personality" has almost completely evaporated has been the difficulty, in large and complex societies (and on examination many "primitive" societies have proven to be very complex, too, especially in their elaborate kinship structures), of identifying cultural patterns in metaphorical and holistic terms. What strikes one, in looking at any society, is the contrasting patterns that seemingly exist at the same time, or succeed each other so as to question the stability of a culture pattern. Thus, in reading travelers' accounts of England, one is told that the English are practical, matter-of-fact, and utilitarian and that they are law-abiding and well-behaved; yet other accounts will emphasize the romanticism and tradition-bound nature of English life, its conservatism, and still others will center on the boisterousness and roistering of the squirearchy and gentry. Each may be a partial perspective, or each of the generalizations may be true of a particular period of time. But a generalization, to make sense, or to be scientific, must be invariant, that is, must hold true for a sustained period, or else one has to know the principle of change. Either the generalizations are wrong, or we do not know the principle of change.

In a different sense, the Parsonian scheme has proven to be too formalistic. It is a very comprehensive grid and gives us a vocabulary of analysis, but in and of itself it is too removed from an empirical or historical reality to give us a point of re-entry. From a different point of view, this writer, in *The Cultural Contradictions of Capitalism* (1976), has questioned whether one can look at a society in holistic terms. The argument put forth is that societies are disjunctive, for two reasons. One is that, if one looks at the economic, political, and cultural realms, each is ruled by different axial principles that often are antagonistic to each other. Thus, in modern Western societies, the economy is ruled by a principle of efficiency, specialization, and maximization, in which individuals are treated, segmentally, in terms of their roles. The axial structure is bureaucratization. In the polity, however, the axial principle is equality—equality before the law, equality of opportunity, and even, in some demands, equality of outcomes, while the structural principle is one of participation. Inherently, there is a tension between bureaucracy and participation, and this tension has framed Western society for the past seventy years. The axial principle of culture is that of self-realization and, at the extreme, self-gratification, and this emphasis on being considered a whole person, and the hedonism which the culture promotes, clashes with the efficiency principle and even with the work ethic of the economy.

If one looks at social change, there is a different disjunction. In the techno-economic realm, there is a "linear" principle, because of the clear rule of substitution: if a machine, a tool, or a product is cheaper, better, more efficient or extracts more energy, one uses this in place of the previous item. But in culture there is no linear principle, or even no "progress." Boulez does not replace Bach; the two coexist. Culture widens the moral and expressive repertoire of mankind. Yet, if this is true, then culture and economics do not match, and the idea of thinking of civilizations as wholes, of a Greek or Roman or modern world, in Hegel's terms, or the successive modes of production in Marx's scheme of social evolution, or the various Spenglerian or Toynbean terms, is wrong. If this theory of disjunctions is true, we need different schemes to group together different time periods of history.

Efforts to use social science for policy purposes have come up against methodological, as well as evident political, difficulties. In the area of social indicators, a major problem is conceptual. If one asks, as I did earlier, whether a country is healthier or not, what does one mean by "health"? The quick and conventional response is that people live longer. But the difficulty with that answer is that the longer the individual lives, the greater the marginal increment of time spent in hospitals, and medical costs, thus, go up even higher. How does one aggregate different diseases and illnesses along a single dimension? In a realistic sense, one cannot. Economics is relatively simpler because one can, as I pointed out earlier, convert apples and pears, potatoes and automobiles to a single metric—money—and weight the units. But what metric is available for health, and how does one weight the different components? Or, if we ask whether there is more crime or less in the country, what then? It would seem to be a simple problem. Yet—apart from the crimes that are not reported—the conceptual question is how does one aggregate and weight the number of murders, rapes, assaults, thefts, burglaries, and so forth into a single index? One way is to adopt "shadow prices." In the case of crime, it would be "time." How many years in jail does a murderer get, a rapist, a burglar, etc.? The difficulty here is the variability of the sentencing. So, for conceptual reasons, social indicators have not fared so well in recent years.

Social forecasting has encountered a different order of difficulty. This can be best understood by making a distinction, somewhat arbitrary to be sure, between prediction and forecasting. Prediction is an effort to identify a spot or a single event: who will win a next election? who will succeed Brezhnev? will the Chilean dictatorship fall? But since such events are subject to so many contingencies or imponderables, prediction is rarely possible or, if it is, it is a function of close intelligence, or of inside information. Social forecasting is the effort to establish relevant social frameworks, or major structural relationships, so that one can stipulate what kinds of problems may arise in a succeeding time period.

Some of these frameworks are demographic. Thus, we know that in almost all of Latin America, Asia, and Africa, the proportion of individuals under seventeen years of age is between 40 and 50 percent of the population. In the Western industrialized countries, the proportion is between 20 and 27 percent. What this would indicate—and one can take Mexico as a prime example—is that in the next decade there will be a doubling of the entry rate into the labor force or into the higher schools similar to the bulge of young people which swept through the Western countries in the 1960s. How will that economy absorb that large new cohort of young persons? Or, in the Soviet Union, we know that the birth rate in the Asian areas is almost twice that of the European areas. Within a decade and a half, the Russians will be in a minority within the Soviet Union. Three out of every ten Soviet soldiers will be Moslem. How will the Soviet planners meet this problem? Will they seek to bring the large, surplus populations from Central Asia to European Russia, risking ethnic tensions as a consequence? Or will they site new plants and equipment in the Asian areas, thus creating huge new problems of capital investment and risking the loss of political controls? In short, we can identify problems, but we do not know what the responses, largely political, will be.

In a different set of social frameworks, we can show that in the Western societies there is a move away from manufacturing, or the production of goods, to services, just as in the previous fifty years there was a move away from agriculture to industry. In the United States, for example, it is likely that, by the year 2000, only 10 percent of the labor force will be industrial workers. If this seems low, the fact is that today only 17 percent of the labor force is engaged in factory work, and, given the introduction of microprocessors and numerical control machine tools into production, the rate of displacement may quicken. If 10 percent seems low, who might have predicted, fifty years ago, that only 4 percent of the U.S. labor force today would be in agriculture, producing food for the United States and for other parts of the world as well? Thus, the shift from an industrial to a post-industrial framework is a shift in the structural arrangements of society.

The limits of social science

If one reflects on the promises and disappointments of the social sciences in the quarter century since the end of World War II, it should not be a counsel for despair, but a realization of the limits of a *social* science. One can put it in these formal terms:

a) A theory or a model is, necessarily, a simplification of reality. No theory or model can completely represent a multifarious reality in all its diversity and variety. To think that one can do this is to be guilty of what A. N. Whitehead called "the fallacy of misplaced concreteness." To that extent, any theory is inherently bound to be somewhat inadequate in dealing with a specific reality, especially a social reality.

b) A science — any science — can only deal with classes of events, not with particulars. And a science can find the reality it is dealing with more tractable to the extent that it is abstract, homogeneous, with properties stable in linear terms, since the mathematics of nonlinear equations is extremely limited. The simplicity of physics or chemistry is that it deals with elements that are homogeneous within any class, since the chemical properties of any molecule of water are the same for every other molecule of water. But social science questions often hinge on particular situations or particular events, such as the will and character of individuals. As Sidney Hook pointed out in *The Hero in History* (1943), there are "event-making" men, and it is not true that events always cast up the right man at the right time. Without the iron will of Lenin, it is not necessarily true that the October Revolution would have happened. If Charles de Gaulle had not replaced the weak Guy Mollet and Mollet's weak successors as premier of France in 1958, the revolt of the French Army in Algeria against the French government might have taken a successful course.

c) Most events, even in the physical world, are not completely deterministic but stochastic, *i.e.*, they involve random or chance probability. We do not live completely in a Newtonian universe, either in the micro-phenomena of quantum physics or in the social world. A new mathematics to deal with probability has developed rapidly in the last several decades. John von Neumann at one point thought that the prediction of weather would be possible because sophisticated computers would be able to compute all the interacting variables in the atmosphere in "real time." Yet as Tjalling C. Koopmans, who won the Nobel Prize in Economics in 1975, has pointed out, beyond a certain threshold the introduction of added complexity makes the resulting answers less and less reliable. Thus, paradoxically, an effort to obtain complete information can be self-defeating.

What have emerged, in the quarter century since the end of World War II, are striking advances in methodology and technique. This has been so in game theory, in decision theory, and in utility theory, all of which are ways of ordering problems and, more importantly, ways of clarifying choices. In economics, there have been advances in cost-benefit analysis and in linear programming (which allows for more rational scheduling, or allocation of tasks). In sociology, there has been the development of multiple regression, which provides the analyst with a technique for sorting out the various background factors which may have entered or affected a result and the amount of variance attributable to each (*e.g.*, if one were charting social mobility, one could seek to assess the relative weights and influence of parents' class, cultural advantages, the years of schooling, family size, IQ, or other factors which might affect an individual's chance to get ahead), and of network analysis, which shows the way "chains of opportunity," or "vacancy chains" (in housing, or in the "bumping" of jobs by seniority in plant lay-offs), affect an entire network or chain of other persons, and the like.

Technique by itself, of course, no matter how sophisticated, is useless if it cannot be applied. And in one sense the advances in methodologies and techniques have outstripped our theories; or, to put it a different way, there is a mismatch in that the theories are not often put, or sometimes cannot be put, in forms that are testable. But one reason has been that, in sociology at least, many of these theories have been put in grand or either/or terms, whereas the problems, when one is closer to the actual terrain, are often not either/or, but how much more or less, or how does one explain the *variations* among persons. If one makes the loose (and, in the end, vacuous) statement that poverty breeds crime, it is best to consider not whether that is true, but who among the poor commit crimes, who do not, and why. Putting forth a proposition or a theory in stark chiaroscuro terms often commands attention, but it is not the most effective way of going about the understanding of a problem.

The first part of this review has attempted to look at the major statements that held promise in the social sciences in the quarter century since the end of World War II. In the 1970s there have been a number of new and significant turns in the social sciences, among them some radical new departures, such as sociobiology, some a breaking apart of economics, and the development of many new approaches, particularly in the field of microeconomics. In sociology, we have seen a revival of neo-Marxism and a turn to hermeneutics, or interpretative sociology, as against the positivism of a previous period. And in psychology and anthropology, there has been an upsurge of structuralism, in the new appreciation of Jean Piaget and the starburst emergence of Claude Lévi-Strauss as a major figure. It is with these developments that Part Two will deal.

---

[1] Karl W. Deutsch, John Platt, and Dieter Senghaas, "Conditions Favoring Major Advances in Social Science," *Science*, 5 February 1971, Vol. 171, no. 3970, pp. 450-59. (Quotations from p. 450.)

[2] Paul A. Samuelson, "Economics in a Golden Age: A Personal Memoir," in *The Twentieth-Century Sciences*, ed. Gerald Holton (New York: W. W. Norton, 1972) pp. 155-70. (Quotations from pp. 159, 166.) Reprinted also in *The Collected Scientific Papers of Paul A. Samuelson*, eds. Hirokai Nagatami and Kate Crowley (Cambridge, Mass.: MIT Press 1977) pp. 881-96.

[3] Ibid. (Holton, p. 160).

[4] George T. Guilband, *What Is Cybernetics?*, trans. Valerie MacKay (New York: Grove Press, 1960), pp. 5-6. I am indebted to M. Guilband for the references to Plato and Ampère.

[5] Randall L. Dahling, "Shannon's Information Theory: The Spread of an Idea," in *Studies in the Utilization of Behavioral Science*, Vol. II (Institute for Communications Research, Stanford University, 1962). The first popular exposition of Shannon's work, it might be noted, was by Francis Bello, "The Information Theory," in *Fortune*, December 1953.

[6] Noam Chomsky, "The General Properties of Language," in *Brain Mechanisms Underlying Speech and Language*, ed. Frederic L. Darley (New York and London: Grune and Stratton, 1967), p. 81. For Chomsky's discussion of Skinner, *see* review of B. F. Skinner's *Verbal Behavior in Language*, reprinted in *The Structure of Language*, eds. Jerry A. Fodor and Jerrold J. Katz (Englewood Cliffs, N. J.: Prentice-Hall, 1964). Chomsky's *Language and Mind* is his most comprehensive and, for the layman, the clearest statement of his position (New York: Harcourt, Brace & World, 1968).

[7] Stephen Toulmin, "Norbert Wiener and Warren McCulloch," in *Makers of Modern Thought* (New York: American Heritage Publishing Co., 1972), pp. 489-90.

[8] George A. Miller, "The Magical Number Seven, Plus or Minus Two," in *The Psychological Review*, Vol. 63, no. 2, March 1956, pp. 90, 95. Reprinted in George A. Miller, *The Psychology of Communication* (New York: Basic Books, 1967), Chap. 2.

[9] George A. Miller, "Computers, Communication and Cognition," in *The Psychology of Communication*, pp. 112-13, 117.

[10] *See* Marvin Minsky, "Artificial Intelligence," in *Information*, a Scientific American book (San Francisco: W. H. Freeman and Co., 1966), pp. 204-7.

[11] James S. Coleman, "Equal Schools or Equal Students?," *The Public Interest*, no. 4, Summer 1966, pp. 73-74.

[12] Ibid., p. 74.

Part II

In the twenty-five years after World War II, from 1945 to 1970, the social sciences seemed to be on the verge of presenting a set of comprehensive paradigms which would not only provide coherent theoretical schemas to order the bodies of human knowledge but would also provide reliable guides to social policy and planning through the new research techniques and the adoption of mathematical and quantitative modes that hitherto had been associated largely with the physical sciences. The prime example of this was economics. Not only had neoclassical economics (as formulated by Alfred Marshall) become joined to the work of John Maynard Keynes in a new synthesis (associated largely with the name of Paul Samuelson) but the development of new methods of macroeconomic analysis—e.g., the gross national product and national income accounts developed by Simon Kuznets, Colin Clark, and Richard Stone, the input-output matrices of Wassily Leontief, the econometric models by Lawrence Klein, the formulation of linear programming by George Dantzig, and the measurement of technological change by Edward Denison and its integration into economic theory by Robert Solow—all promised the completion of a set of intellectual tools which, as the phrase went, would allow policymakers to "fine tune" the economy.

Other social science developments held out similar promise. The yoking of cybernetics, linguistic theory, cognitive psychology, and computer science seemed to foreshadow a new discipline that could successfully "model" the mind as well as society. Culture and personality theory, initiated by Ruth Benedict, proposed to show how patterns of culture were reflected in modal personality types, and thus to demonstrate the interactions of social behavior. Structural-Functionalism in sociology, a theory identified primarily with Talcott Parsons, sought to build a "general theory" of society by identifying the mechanisms of integration in cultural and social systems. And, in government, the large-scale expenditures in social-policy programs and research indicated an aim to show that social experiments and evaluation of policy could give us a more secure basis of policy judgment on health, education, welfare, housing, manpower training, and interracial issues.

Most of these promises—as discussed in Part One of this essay, in *The Great Ideas Today* 1979—have gone unrealized. In some instances, as in economics, the science became more elegant in its mathematical formula-

55

tions but seemed less able to deal with the more complex socioeconomic reality. The "general systems" approach, as promised by cybernetics and computers, seems to have been too grandiose, and while some important and significant advances have been made in such areas as computer applications to cognitive learning (e.g., the work of Seymour Papert at M.I.T.), the more ambitious claims have been toned down. In anthropology the "culture and personality" emphasis has almost vanished, as subsequent work has shown that the premises were too simplistic, that culture patterns could not be described in "holistic" terms, and that a theory of "personality dynamics" could not be sustained. Structural-Functionalism in sociology, while a towering intellectual effort to provide a complete morphology of society and, in the history of social thought, a major effort to work out the logic of Max Weber and Émile Durkheim through a set of comprehensive categories which could encompass the entire range of social actions, was an effort that many sociologists felt was too abstract and could provide no direct ways to deal with sociographic or empirical issues. And the experiments in social policy, by and large, proved to be failures, though few persons could agree upon the reasons. Some social scientists pointed out, quite justly, that a number of these programs had been trumpeted by the government as "social science" when there was little science in them, either in warranted theory or in reliable data. Conversely, policymakers claimed that the social scientists themselves had been too schematic and abstract in their approaches and had failed to understand the *political* nature of social policy, both as a process in government and in terms of popular reaction. Whatever the reasons—and these will be matters for the historians to adjudicate—the fact remains that a sobering or disillusioning mood began to prevail in this area as well.

In the 1970s the social sciences went off in two divergent directions. On the one hand (if one was pessimistic) one could say that there was a splintering of the fields; or (if one was optimistic) one could say that the social sciences had retreated to more mundane, more empirical, and "smaller," more manageable problems of research, all in the hope eventually of finding some warranted generalizations with which one could reknit the disciplines. In most fields, certainly, there had been significant advances in quantitative modes of research and in sophisticated mathematical tools, and these were now being applied assiduously to trace out in a precise way the specific variables which researchers felt were important in solving their problems. In the sociology of medicine, for example, there have been striking advances in epidemiology that relate the incidence of disease to different segments of populations. And in the study of social mobility, there have been painstaking regression models and path analyses to show exactly how factors such as parent's occupation, cultural advantage, schooling, I.Q., and the like affect the chances of individuals to get ahead in the society. In effect, what has happened has been the spread of "empiricism" and a retreat from grand theory—though critics of these efforts argue that without theory, empiricism can only multiply results endlessly, and that to wait for some "pattern" to emerge is to submit to the fallacy of inductivism.

On the other hand, there were, in the 1970s, major new synoptic attempts to provide some master keys to the understanding of social behavior (it is an incorrigible impulse in science), and these efforts themselves have provoked new and often savage disputes. In this past decade, one can identify four major developments in the social sciences:

(1) The emergence of sociobiology as an effort to unify all social behavior through the parameters, genetically based, that govern kin selection, territoriality, division of labor, group size, etc., through a fusion of ethology, ecology, population genetics, and neo-evolutionary theory.

(2) The multiplicity of new paradigms in macroeconomics in the work of Herbert A. Simon, Harvey Leibenstein, and Thomas Schelling.

(3) New schools of neo-Marxism, bringing forth a plethora of new approaches that, by and large, still bog down in exegetical and textual quarrels as to what Marx "really" said or meant.

(4) Structuralism, a term which is quite diffuse but which has been used to describe the work of Lévi-Strauss in anthropology, Piaget in psychology, Roland Barthes in literature, Louis Althusser in Marxism, Jacques Lacan in psychoanalysis—and a host of epigones who have carried the word into almost every domain of knowledge.

It would be nigh impossible, within a short space, and for a general audience, to survey the myriad number of empirical studies that have sprouted in the social sciences in the last decade, and even more difficult to draw any large generalizations.

What this essay attempts to do is to explore these four developments and to conclude with the question whether the dream of a unified social science or some master system is possible.

1. Sociobiology

In her *Patterns of Culture* (1934), Ruth Benedict set forth the foundations of anthropology, if not of all the social sciences, in terms of two propositions: the uniqueness of the human species, as against other species, in shaping social behavior; and, given the extraordinary diversity of culture patterns, the relativism of culture. She wrote:

> There are societies where Nature perpetuates the slightest mode of
> behaviour by biological mechanisms, but these are societies not of men
> but of the social insects. . . . Not *one* item of his tribal social
> organization, of his language, of his local religion, is carried in his
> germ-cell. . . . Man is not committed in detail by his biological
> constitution to any particular variety of behaviour. The great diversity
> of social solutions that man has worked out in different cultures in
> regard to mating, for example, or trade, are all equally possible on the

basis of his original endowment. . . . We must accept all the
implications of our human inheritance, one of the most important of
which is the small scope of biologically transmitted behaviour, and the
enormous rôle of the cultural process of the transmission of tradition.[1]

Little more than forty years later, a man who had made his reputation
with a powerful book on insect societies, E. O. Wilson of Harvard, brought
forth a new book, *Sociobiology: The New Synthesis* (1975), which promised the
creation of a major new discipline that would relate the social sciences to
biology and explain fundamental patterns of social life through the
theoretical principles of neo-Darwinian evolutionary biology. The premise
of the proposed discipline denied the "uniqueness" of the human species,
accepted the wide variety of human behaviour, but interpreted that diversity in evolutionary terms as a form of species strategy that was consistent with
principles underlying the adaptation of other species. Wilson even
proposed (to take one small example) that homosexuality may be related
to species' adaptive mechanisms, which seek to strengthen the gene pools
of a species. Sociobiology sought to establish two claims: that one could not
ignore the role of biology—in particular, of genetics—in explaining some
fundamental and universal constants of human behavior; and that a unified
theory could explain some constants in group behavior, such as territoriality, sexual mating patterns, aggressive responses, in the chain of evolutionary species, and that aspects of these theories could be applied to human
social behavior when considered in a long evolutionary perspective.

Greeted at first with an acclaim so rapid as to take almost all observers
by surprise, Wilson's work also became the storm center of a controversy
so vehement as to earn a place in the annals of intellectual history. Yet
Sociobiology did not emerge out of the blue. It was, as the subtitle of the work
indicated, an attempt at a new synthesis. Over the previous forty years a
number of new theories and ideas had developed in ethology, ecology, and
population genetics, and it was the effort to derive some underlying principles from all these and give them precise formulation, in many instances
in mathematical form, that gave Wilson's work its distinction. To understand its novelty, and the nature of the controversy, one has to sort out the
intellectual strands in his writings and to clarify the ideological fears they
have aroused.

Traditionally, animal or bird behavior was thought to consist of simple
responses, some of them innate and some learned, to a stimulus or signal,
e.g., an attack, or a courtship signal. But the work of certain ethologists,
notably Konrad Lorenz, Nikolaas Tinbergen, and Karl von Frisch (all of
whom won the Nobel Prize in 1973), established a new view of animal
behavior. They showed that animals have an innate capacity for complex
acts in response to simple stimuli, i.e., that the response is not on a one-to-
one basis, but involves a variety of possible responses, and that certain
behavior patterns are inherited. In other words, genetically determined

responses must be subject to the pressures of natural selection, and innate behavior must evolve. Thus, for example, a motor pattern involved in a context of feeding could evolve into a ritualized form as a signal, as in courtship or an attack; thus it could change from a noncommunicatory act to a communicatory act, presumably under the selective pressures of the environment; and these new, adaptive patterns would then be utilized by later biological members of the species.

In a different context, the Scottish ecologist V. C. Wynne-Edwards published a book in 1962, *Animal Dispersion in Relation to Social Behaviour*, in which he suggested, as David Barash put it, that virtually all social behavior— including dominance hierarchies, securing of territories, flocking in birds, herding in mammals—are regulatory devices to relate population levels of the group to the ecological limits in the availability of food. Barash writes: "It had long been recognized that socially subordinate individuals often fail to breed and that overpopulation in nature is rare. Wynne-Edwards suggested that social congregations serve to inform individuals of the local population density, so that individuals could avoid overpopulation by regulating their own breeding accordingly."*

The weakness of many of these ethological studies, however, is that they are based on naturalistic observation and do not explain the way innate behavior evolved, i.e., the genetic mechanisms. Moreover, as the influential book of George C. Williams, *Adaptation and Natural Selection: A Critique of Some Current Evolutionary Thought* (1966), points out, natural selection has to explain how the process operates not through the group but through the individual, since it is the individual who transmits the genetic pattern. This problem becomes the bridge to the next strand.

This second strand is the work in population genetics that began in the 1940s and is summed up in the neo-Darwinism associated with Theodosius Dobzhansky, George Gaylord Simpson, and Ernst Mayr. (It is summed up in Mayr's magisterial book, *Populations, Species, and Evolution* [1970].) Classical Darwinism was based on two postulates: the idea of the common descent of all mammals, including man, from one ancestral species, in a long chain of being; and the idea of natural selection, to explain the enormous variation of species, as an adaptive mechanism to the environment. But Darwin had no notion of the source or mechanism of variation, of the way in which hereditary information is transmitted from parent to offspring through the genes. Mendel made his discoveries in 1865, but these were largely ignored or unknown until rediscovered in 1900.

The new Darwinian synthesis, or neo-Darwinism, as it is now called, starts out with the uniquely different individuals who are organized into interbreeding populations. Given this premise, every biological individual has a dual component: the *genotype* (the full component of genes, not all of which may be expressed) and the *phenotype* (the observable properties of the

---

* *The Wilson Quarterly*, Summer 1977, pp. 109–10.

organism, as they have developed out of the genetic inheritance *and* the responses to the environment). The genotype is part of the gene pool of a specific interbreeding population, but it is the individual, the phenotype, that competes with other phenotypes for reproductive success.

Not only is the emphasis on the individual, or phenotype, central, but the very concept of the species as a fixed *type*, qualitatively distinct from other types, is called into question. Every interbreeding population—called a *deme*—is a statistical distributed set of genes in the gene pool, a set of variations, the "cluster" of which, or the statistical "mean," is an abstraction, since only the variant individual has reality. The importance of the gene pool lies in the distribution of variations, but it is the success or failure of the single individual that "advances" the different traits in the gene pool. As Mayr writes:

> In a population of thousands or millions of unique individuals some will have sets of genes that are better suited to the currently prevailing assortment of ecological pressures. Such individuals will have a statistically greater probability of surviving and of leaving survivors than other members of the population. It is this . . . step in natural selection that determines evolutionary direction, increasing the frequency of genes and constellations of genes that are adaptive at a given time and place, increasing fitness, promoting specialization and giving rise to adaptive radiation and to what may be loosely described as evolutionary progress.[2]

Classical Darwinian theory held that every organism fights for its own survival, and the chance to reproduce. But that theory could not explain why some organisms help other members of their kind. A prairie dog barks when it sees a predator. The alarm gives the other dogs a signal and a chance to escape but calls attention to the animal that utters it and thus reduces its chances of survival. How does one explain this "altruistic" action? A solution was proposed in 1964 in two articles by the British geneticist W. D. Hamilton ("The Genetical Theory of Social Behaviour," in the *Journal of Theoretical Biology,* vol. 7, 1964). Hamilton pointed out that "altruistic behavior" is actually a case of ensuring the survival of those who share *common* genes. Natural selection is supplemented by "kin selection," i.e., the occurrence of altruistic behavior increases with the closeness of the beneficiary: the more genes that are shared by common ancestry, the more likely does behavior tend to be altruistic. Hamilton's work predicted that altruistic and cooperative behavior would be found more frequently in the interactions of related than of unrelated individuals, and this has been confirmed by observation. Thus, evolutionary adaptation takes place not by the survival of the individual but through the efforts of kin, apparently genetically motivated, to ensure the survival of their close kind.

This addition of the theory of kin selection made possible a closer fit between evolutionary behavior and social theory and gave biologists a bridge from insect societies to primates and, they have argued, to human behavior.* And while kin selection is the most dramatic innovation, providing the third major strand, there are still other bridges that biologists have proposed to span the range of social behavior in studies of territoriality, mating systems, and communication as basic social phenomena.

Sociobiology is the effort to provide this synthesis. As Wilson remarks in his book:

> Biologists have always been intrigued by comparisons between societies of invertebrates, especially insect societies, and those of vertebrates. They have dreamed of identifying the common properties of such disparate units in a way that would provide insight into all aspects of social evolution, including that of man. The goal can be expressed in modern terms as follows: *when the same parameters and quantitative theory are used to analyze both termite colonies and troops of rhesus macaques, we will have a unified science of sociobiology.* (p. 4, emphasis added)

Wilson admits that such comparison may be facile, and a deliberate oversimplification, but he points out how impressed he has been with the functional similarities between insect societies and troops of monkeys. He writes:

> Consider for a moment termites and monkeys. Both are formed into cooperative groups that occupy territories. The group members communicate hunger, alarm, hostility, caste status or rank, and reproductive status among themselves by means of something on the order of 10 to 100 nonsyntactical signals. Individuals are intensely aware of the distinction between groupmates and nonmembers. Kinship plays an important role in group structure and probably served as a chief generative force of sociality in the first place. In both kinds of society there is a well-marked division of labor....

Sociobiology, as Wilson outlines it, would deal with the effective population size of groups with common genetic features, and the nature of the gene flow between them. "The principal goal of a general theory of sociobiology," he writes, "should be an ability to predict features of social organization from a knowledge of these population parameters combined with information on the behavioral constraints imposed by the genetic constitution of the species."

In his book of more than 600 double-column text pages, Wilson explored every form of animal society from machinelike colonies of jellyfish to

---

* As Hamilton points out, the highest degree of cooperation is displayed by colonies of genetically identical cells that make up the human body. And as John Maynard Smith comments:

"It is important to note that these concepts apply to organisms incapable of recognizing degrees of relationship. In species that usually live in family groups a gene causing an individual to act altruistically towards members of its own community will increase in frequency even if the individuals carrying it cannot recognize family members."

screeching chimpanzees, dealing with topics from time-energy budgets to mating patterns and kin selection, all in twenty-six chapters. The twenty-seventh chapter dealt with man. Admitting the much greater degree of plasticity of human social organization, Wilson, more tentatively, also insisted that one could raise the question whether there might be genetic predispositions for both class position and religion, since individuals "are absurdly easy to indoctrinate — they *seek* it." In a later book, *On Human Nature* (1978), Wilson restates the issue in more general but stronger terms. He writes: "if the genetic components of human nature did not originate by natural selection, fundamental evolutionary theory is in trouble. At the very least the theory of evolution would have to be altered to account for a new and as yet unimagined form of genetic change in populations. Consequently, an auxiliary goal of human sociobiology is to learn whether the evolution of human nature conforms to conventional evolutionary theory." (pp. 33–34)

The criticism of the sociobiology project has been both ideological and intellectual. The first arose in left-wing and liberal circles that feared sociobiology would become an ideology for racism and conservatism, as an aspect of Social Darwinism had been in the late nineteenth and early twentieth centuries. There were several reasons for the fear. In the previous decade and a half, works popularizing some of the findings in ethology, such as Robert Ardrey's *African Genesis* (1961) and *The Territorial Imperative* (1966), as well as Desmond Morris's *The Naked Ape* (1967), had argued that aggression, territoriality, and hierarchy (i.e., the pecking order in animals) were innate or "natural," and that utopian or liberal ideas about the possibility of changing human nature were fallacious. More to the point, a number of psychologists had begun to argue that achievement in school was due primarily to I.Q. and that remedial and other programs for the disadvantaged might fail or be costly unless this fact were taken into account. The psychologist Arthur Jensen argued that there was a distinct difference in the modal scores of black and white populations. Richard Herrnstein sought to place the problem not on the basis of group or race but simply of differences in I.Q. and argued that 80 percent of an individual's I.Q. is derived from inheritance (technically, in any large group of persons, 80 percent of the variance could be attributed to genetic inheritance), so that if social standing were equalized, or a policy of equality of result created by government policies were instituted, those with the higher I.Q. would come to occupy higher positions in society.

The introduction of the I.Q. issue, the debate on school achievement and equality, and the allegations of the schools' failure to improve the standing of minority and disadvantaged children all combined to rouse in liberal and left groups the fear that biological arguments were being used to justify cuts in governmental social programs and to subtly introduce questions of racial inferiority. While it is true that some conservatives did raise the question of genetic incapability as a reason for attacking Great Society programs, the validity of the sociobiology argument became, for a while, almost hopelessly entangled in these political and ideological questions.

The intellectual case for or against the claims of sociobiology to embrace social behavior within the framework of neo-Darwinian principles rests on three theoretical issues. One is the question whether the principle of kin selection in its strong forms operates within human groups as it does within other species; two, the question whether the variability of human cultures is a function of a distinctively new principle of consciousness; and three, related to the second but possessing logical autonomy, the question whether, even if there were shown to be some genetic foundations for specific behavioral patterns, the biological "level of explanation" is not more adequate to explain behavior than psychology and sociology—technically, the question of "reductionism."

The fundamental calculus of sociobiology—the adaptive role of kin selection—is based on the proposition that, as Wilson has put it, a person has 50 percent of his genes held in common with a full sibling and that altruistic behavior by that sibling would favor those genes, so that "the altruistic genes will spread through the population." The calculus has been attacked by S. L. Washburn, who writes:

> A parent does not share one half of the genes with its offspring; the offspring shares one half of the genes in which the parents differ. If the parents are homozygous for a gene, obviously all offspring will inherit that gene. The issue then becomes, How many shared genes are there within a species such as *Homo Sapiens*? . . . Individuals whom sociobiologists consider unrelated share, in fact, more than 99 percent of their genes. It would be easy to make a model in which the structure and physiology important in behavior are based on the shared 99% and in which behaviorally unimportant differences, such as hair form, are determined by the 1%.*

And Marshall Sahlins, the cultural anthropologist, has argued that kinship behavior in human societies does not follow the genetic calculus, that "marriage rules" are highly variable, and that genetic sharing decreases far more rapidly than social obligations in any human social system.

In one sense, the parties to the debate are talking past each other. The sociobiologists tend to look for what they regard as universals in human culture and seek to root these in some kind of genetic predisposition. The anthropologists concentrate on the wide variety of human traits. Thus, in *On Human Nature,* Wilson cites a study by the anthropologist George P. Murdock that lists almost eighty activities, from age-grading to weather control, "that have been recorded in every culture known to history and ethnography," while the anthropologist Marvin Harris, in an attack on sociobiology, states: "George Peter Murdock's *World Ethnographic Atlas* con-

---

* "Human Behavior and the Behavior of Other Animals," *American Psychologist*, May 1978, p. 415.

tains forty-six columns of variable cultural traits. Over a thousand variable components per society can be identified by using the alternative codes listed under these columns. No two societies in the sample of 1,179 have the same combination of components."*

To put the question as culture versus biology, however, is not only wrong but misleading. The more difficult question is: in what way does genetic inheritance limit the ranges of human behavior; or again, in what way does genetic predisposition facilitate what kinds of change? In short, what does the human "biogram" allow us to do or not to do?

Wilson accepts the idea of variability. In his *Sociobiology* he writes: "The parameters of social organization, including group size, properties of hierarchies, and rates of gene exchange, vary far more among human populations than among those of any other primate species. The variation exceeds even that occurring between the remaining primate species." But he then goes on to argue: "The hypothesis to consider, then, is that genes promoting flexibility in social behavior are strongly selected at the individual level. But note that variation in social organization is only a possible, not a necessary consequence of this process." And, in fact, in *On Human Nature* Wilson concludes: "I believe that a correct application of evolutionary theory also favors diversity in the gene pool as a cardinal virtue. If variation in mental and athletic ability is influenced to a moderate degree by heredity, as the evidence suggests, we should expect individuals of truly extraordinary capacity to emerge unexpectedly in otherwise undistinguished families...."

If the argument were left only on the "species" level, there would probably have been little dispute and little excitement over sociobiology. Where the issue becomes more problematic is the effort of many sociobiologists to specify gene-controlled behavior traits that are shared with Old World primates, and gene-controlled behavior traits that are specific to human beings. Wilson, for example, mentions incest avoidance, male bonding, territoriality, semantic symbol language that develops in the young on a relatively strict timetable, specific facial expressions and other features as genetically restricted, and insists that "to socialize a human being out of such species-specific traits would be very difficult if not impossible, and almost certainly destructive to mental development."† It is in the definition of such "species-specific traits," and the exact degree of determinism, that the intellectual heat of the debate has centered.

The issue of reductionism is a double one. In one dimension it is the fear that sociobiology will deflate man by seeing behavior as either genetically predisposed or as a strategy to enhance one's own kind of genes. As Wilson, who is a scientific materialist, has said: "We are likely to see some of our

---

* *Cultural Materialism: The Struggle for a Science of Culture* (New York: Random House, 1979), p. 124.

† Edward O. Wilson, "Biology and the Social Sciences," *Daedalus*, vol. 2 (Fall 1977), p. 132.

most exalted feelings explained in terms of traits which evolved. We may find that there is an overestimation of the nature of our deepest yearnings."

The second aspect of reductionism is more methodological and goes to the core of some central questions in the philosophy of science: namely, whether the level of explanation of a sociological question (e.g., the kinds and varieties of human groups, or the layout of roads, or the patterns of exchange between persons) is fully answerable in sociological terms, or whether such an answer requires, as well, the "reduction" of that explanation to psychological levels (e.g., of individual motivations and desires) and of that, in turn, to biological levels of genetic codes—some writers (e.g., Francis Crick) arguing that biological explanations themselves have to be reduced to physical-chemical laws.

Wilson has argued the need for some kind of biological reductionism. He has written:

> The full phenomenology of social life cannot be predicted from a knowledge of the genetic programs of the individuals alone. When the observer shifts his attention from one level of organization to the next, *he expects to find obedience to all of the laws of the levels* below. But upper levels of organization require specification of the arrangement of the lower units, which in turn generates richness and the basis of new and unexpected principles. The specification can be classified into three categories: combinatoric, spatial, and historical.[3]

Yet, as the anthropologist Clifford Geertz has pointed out, the reductionist approach inherent in sociobiology—which seeks to explain human social behavior in terms of broad principles applicable to ants as well as to humans—is derived from a defective philosophy of science, based on a hierarchical concept of disciplines. Geertz has proposed thinking of these questions in "parallel" terms, and in his inimitable way he has offered "clowning" as an example. A clown's skill is a disposition, which depends upon certain kinds of neurological complexities and muscular developments, and, since some aspects of facial expressions may be genetically determined (though whether it would be possible to ascertain this is another matter), biologists could provide some understanding. At the same time, clowning might be discussed in the psychoanalytical context as tendencies to exhibitionism. Or, in the context of social institutions, as implying that circuses are a social mode to play out roles. Or, in connection with certain cultural traditions, as an instance of modes that mimic clumsiness. As Geertz points out, one can discuss the various aspects of clowning behavior and increase one's understanding of its varied meanings without making any claims to higher or lower levels of explanation.[4]

For all the furor, it is quite clear that in the next decade the relation of biology to the social sciences will become more intimate. One can seek, as the sociobiologists do, for the broad principles that underlie some presumed constants of all living group behavior. Or one can focus, as anthropology does, on the relation of cultural evolution to biological evolution. As Marvin Harris has put it: "It took billions of years for natural selection to create specialized adaptations for fishing, hunting, agriculture; for aquatic, terrestrial, and aerial locomotion; and for predatory and defensive weaponry, such as teeth, claws and armor. Equivalent specialties were developed by cultural evolution in less than ten thousand years. The main focus of human sociobiology ought therefore to be the explanation of why other species have such minuscule and insignificant cultural repertories and why humans alone have such gigantic and important ones."*

Wilson himself agrees in the concluding sentences to his essay on "Biology and the Social Sciences" that "Biology is the key to human nature, and social scientists cannot afford to ignore its emerging principles." He adds, however, that "the social sciences are potentially far richer in content. Eventually they will absorb the relevant ideas of biology and go on to beggar them by comparison."

2. Economics

The regnant "paradigm" in economics in the quarter of a century after World War II was Keynesianism, a doctrine which, in the large, asserted that government intervention could manage the economy through fiscal policy. In the 1970s the consensus as to this had fallen apart. The rock on which that paradigm broke, as Sir John Hicks, the Nobel laureate, sought to show in *The Crisis in Keynesian Economics* (1974), was inflation. But more was at stake for the science itself than the embarrassment of being unable to deal with the most crucial public-policy issue facing a society. What the new discussions brought back into question were the fundamental relationships of analysis and the fundamental terms of inquiry: the fundamental relationship between microeconomics, or the behavior of individuals (with the firm seen as an individual), and macroeconomics, or the aggregates in the economy as a whole; the fundamental terms of "equilibrium," or the idea that relationships between basic variables (e.g., wages-prices, consumption-investment) return to some balance after markets are cleared of a "natural growth rate" for an economy, and the idea of "maximization," or that rational behavior can be defined by saying that individuals do act to optimize their gains and will choose that path of action which will achieve the greatest gain.

The classical framework of analysis of equilibrium began with Say's Law of Markets, which, crudely put, states that "supply creates its own demand." The idea that inadequate demand could be a cause of unemployment was unlikely, since human wants were deemed to be insatiable, and supply would generate the demand through the circular flow of payments from

---

* *Cultural Materialism*, p. 125.

suppliers to consumers or investors. Temporary gluts or shortfalls might always occur, but this would be adjusted through the movements of wages and prices for each market. Neoclassical economists, following Marshall, refined the explanation of Say's Law by using marginal analysis to show the determination of the level of real output. A producer would never seek to offer a worker a wage greater than the value of the added output his labor could produce, so that the number of workers hired by a firm would be set at the point where the marginal cost would equal the marginal output. And by the same reasoning, as John Bates Clark sought to show in his *Distribution of Wealth* (1899), the same principle would apply to the markets for all factors of production, not only to wages but to rents and returns of capital (interest and profit) as well. Clark's "conclusion was that under perfect competition each factor would inexorably receive a return precisely equal to its contribution, and Clark could demonstrate that each factor would receive a [return] equal to the value of the marginal product."[5]

If a money wage was too high, competitive pressure would drive that wage down to the price where the employer would be able to hire a person; if money wages were "sticky," an employer would not hire workers so that unemployment was a "partial equilibrium" at those levels.

In neoclassical theory, a cut in money wages was the same as a cut in real wages because the price level remained unchanged. The level of money wages did not determine the price level, but vice versa. The price level itself (i.e., the *general* price level) was determined by the quantity theory of money, which was accepted by every neoclassical writer. (The prices for individual commodities, i.e., relative prices, might fluctuate for natural or exogenous reasons, from droughts for food, to cartels for oil.) So long as the total quantity of money was held steady, the general price level could not rise, though individual prices, of course, would adjust to each other, under the general "ceiling" conditions. (Thus, having to spend more for fuel oil would force a cut in the spending on some other products.) But almost all neoclassical economists—indeed, the thought goes back to David Hume—believed in the rough proportionality between changes in the stock of money and changes in the general level of prices in the economy.

The neoclassicists made a fundamental distinction between the *real* value of money and the *nominal* value. The real value expresses the actual magnitudes the money can command (tangible items, such as houses, or capital plant, or art works), or what the money can buy in the marketplace. Nominal value is simply the amount of money expressed in a monetary unit, such as the dollar. (To be a "millionaire" would not mean much if a million dollars only bought a cup of coffee, as happened with the German mark in the 1920s.) The general price level is a nominal magnitude. Quantity theorists argued that people act to maintain some level of *real* balances. If the relation between the nominal and the real balances moved out of line, prices would rise (because people would seek to lower their holdings of money) until the nominal money balances would be equal in real terms to the desired or customary level of real balances. In short, a fall in the value of money as prices rose, or a rise in real income, would return the system to equilibrium.

The relation between money, prices, and income was described in a "transactions" model by the American economist Irving Fisher, and in a "cash-balance" method by the neoclassicists at Cambridge. A crucial modification of the monetarist argument was made by the Swedish economist Knut Wicksell, who argued that money could not be treated purely as a commodity, as the cash-balance approach did. He emphasized the growing role of credit and indicated the mechanism by which changes in the quantity of money influenced interest rates, which, in turn, influenced flows of investment and savings. Wicksell thus showed how the interest rate became the equilibrating instrument for the supply and demand for capital.

The neoclassical economists understood that there were often sharp price fluctuations in the real world, and that purely monetary or nominal events, such as a big gold strike, could have real effects in the short run. But they believed that such economic fluctuations were transient, or that monetary distortions after a while would leach away, since underneath these top-of-the-wave turbulences was a basic equilibrium mechanism. The logic of market-oriented equilibrium economics was, if perturbations occurred, to let them run their course, since adjustments (even at times painful ones) would "wring out" the excesses.

Keynesian theory introduced a number of substantial modifications in neoclassical theory. One was the observation that the perturbations, or transient deviations from the equilibrium, could last a long time and have devastating social effects. And, even where there was unemployment or excess capacity in an economy, as in a depression, the price levels were more or less "sticky," and nominal levels therefore had a substantial impact on real quantities. Under full employment, the divorce between nominal events and real quantities would return. Once all capacity, plant and labor, was utilized, additional nominal expenditure would then raise the price levels, and the control of inflation would then be in the power of the monetary authorities to expand or limit the money supply, in order to compress the nominal levels back to the "real" price levels.

In short, what the Keynesians argued was that "natural" equilibrium would not take place in the market economy (or, if it did, it would be at a "partial equilibrium" of high unemployment or unused capacity) and that government fiscal policy intervention was necessary to redress the balance. Inflation was not seen as an issue because inflation was not seen as deriving from a rise in nominal money wages beyond the real price level.

The missing equation in this picture of the relation of wage levels to unemployment and inflation was the famous Phillips Curve, which, as Robert Solow has wryly observed, provided more employment for economists, after its results were published in 1958, than any public-works enterprise since the construction of the Erie Canal. A. W. Phillips, an economist at the

London School of Economics, had matched unemployment rates in Britain between 1862 and 1957 with changes in hourly wage rates. Solow has described its import:

> Notice that he was comparing the rate of change of wages, a nominal quantity, with the percentage of the labor force out of work, a real quantity. If there were no long-run connection between real events and nominal events, then there ought to be no relation between those two time series. If the crude dichotomy in the Keynesian picture were a good description of the world, then the rate of wage inflation ought to be near zero for anything but full employment. And in times of full employment, if there were any to be observed, there ought to be substantial inflation.
>
> What Phillips found was really pretty astonishing. The simple bivariate relation, relating only one real and one nominal variable, held up very well over a very long time during which the nature of British industry and labor changed very drastically. Here was evidence for a strong, and apparently reliable, relation between the nominal world and the real world. It did not appear to be a short-run transient affair, as the mainstream macroeconomics of the 19th and early 20th centuries would have suggested. It seemed not to be a simple dichotomy between less-than-full employment and full employment, as the casual picture of the early 1950s might have suggested. It seemed to say quite clearly that the rate of wage inflation—and probably, therefore, the rate of price inflation—was a smooth function of the tightness of the aggregate economy.[6]

Phillips's study had been a "straight" empirical one. But the theoretical implications for public policy—and for Keynesian economics—were worked out by Paul Samuelson and Robert M. Solow. In their article "Analytical Aspects of Anti-Inflation Policy," in the *American Economic Review* of May 1960, the two M.I.T. economists assembled an analogous time series for the United States. While there were divergences, the postwar data did show a "curve" of the same qualitative shape, and Samuelson and Solow posited a hypothetical relation between the rate of price inflation and the unemployment rate: "This shows the menu of choice between different levels of unemployment and price stability as roughly estimated from the last twenty-five years of American data," they wrote.

The relation known as the Phillips Curve, and its generalization by Richard Lipsey, won immediate and widespread acceptance in American economic thinking. It served, as Franco Modigliani has put it, "to dispose of the rather sterile 'cost-push'–'demand-pull' controversy." It also served to reinforce the idea that one could now "manage" the economy even more decisively because of the "menu" of choice. But the inflation of the 1970s, and especially of the last five years, which have been double-digit years for the most part, has proved recalcitrant to public policy and is a difficult problem for the Keynesian economists.

One can point to a number of specific "perturbations" which conjoined to create this inflation. In the United States the Johnson administration during the Vietnam War had stepped up government spending but refused to compensate for the military expenditures by higher taxes. The "oil shock" of 1973 and after quadrupled and then quintupled energy prices. A series of crop failures in the Soviet Union pushed up food prices. A worldwide synchronization of rising demand and a shortage in primary processing capacity conjoined in the early 1970s. The simultaneity of all these events burst the twenty-five-year worldwide economic expansion which had more than doubled world industrial output.

But in the resulting recession, and in the slow but steady recovery in the U.S., *both* a high level of inflation and an unacceptable level of unemployment have persisted. That is the great theoretical—and seemingly insuperable—puzzle. To put the question within the framework we have been discussing, the Phillips Curve has gone flat, and the idea of a trade-off—of reducing inflation by increasing unemployment, or increasing jobs at the cost of more inflation, the "menu of choice"—has seemingly vanished. As Robert Solow points out in his 1979 essay:

> Most of the serious estimates suggest that an extra 1 percent of unemployment maintained for one year would reduce the rate of inflation by something between 0.16 and 0.5 percent. That trade-off is not very favorable. We also know that the inflationary process involves a great deal of inertia; that is, it takes a long time for the economy to pass from one member of the family of Phillips curves to a lower one, at least under normal circumstances. For instance, an extra 1 percent of unemployment maintained for three years would reduce the inflation rate by something between 0.5 and 1.75 percent. (An extra point of unemployment for three years costs the economy about $180 billion of production, which makes this a very expensive way to reduce the inflation rate.)
>
>   We know those two things, albeit in a tentative and gingerly way. What we don't know ... is why the inertia is so great, why those Phillips Curves are so flat. That is, we do not know what bits of our social and economic structure would have to be changed in order to change those relationships. (Ibid., pp. 44–45)

The inadequacies of Keynesian macroeconomic policy have produced two divergent responses. One is a swing back to monetarist theory. Its argument is that given a constant money supply or a fixed rate of expansion in accordance with business activity, equilibrium forces *will* reassert themselves. It seeks to minimize government intervention, in particular those by the Federal Reserve Board to "time" the expansion or contraction of money in order to affect the price level.

The other response has been that of the "post-Keynesians" and is built on the theoretical work of such Keynes associates as Joan Robinson and

Piero Sraffa, as well as the Polish economist Michal Kalecki, who, independent of Keynes, had come to similar conclusions.

The monetarist argument has been identified principally with Milton Friedman, a Nobel laureate and the leader of the so-called Chicago School. Friedman opened his attack in 1967 in his presidential address to the American Economics Association, in which he reasserted the distinction between real and nominal magnitudes, emphasized the "permanent income hypothesis" (i.e., the idea of "real balances" as the basis of monetary theory), and attacked the Phillips Curve hypothesis. Friedman restated the argument that changes in the quantity of money caused output and price changes, and that in the short run the stock of money was not a neutral reflector of varying demands but a determinant of such demands.

Friedman's major policy prescription was that the monetary authorities, once they have wrung out the excess money in the system (by reducing the money supply or having the government reduce its own spending, which he regards as a prime source of inflation), should set a fixed level of money, plus an additional growth rate, say three percent, consonant with the "natural growth" potential of the society. Within that framework, individuals and firms would make their own self-adjusting decisions, based on relative prices, for their own needs and wants. But, through the control of the quantity of money, the general price level would be kept relatively stable.

A number of questions emerge about the Friedman prescriptions. One has to do with the definitions of money itself. The stock of money is usually calculated in terms of two measures: M-1, or cash in circulation plus money in checking accounts, and M-2, which is M-1 plus time deposits, such as savings accounts and negotiable certificates of deposit by corporations and banks. The argument is that the structural change in the nature of the credit system (from the spread of interest-bearing checking accounts to the volatility of credit because of easily available credit cards), plus the large "overhang" of Euro-dollars—that is, the several hundred billions of U.S. dollars that float around outside the United States and are used as a basis for new dollar loans by foreign banks—all make the question of monetary measurement more difficult and variable.

A second, and perhaps greater, difficulty is that there seems to be an "uncoupling" between money supply and interest rates, so that business behavior seemingly is less affected by these controls than has been assumed. As Lester Thurow has pointed out:

> Business investment functions are probably the best example of this phenomenon. In classical economic theory, rising interest rates lead to less investment and falling interest rates lead to more investment.
> Much to the shock of initial investigators, econometric equations found either no effect or the exact opposite to be true. Investment was not

affected or went up when interest rates went up. Econometricians immediately went back to their computers to find an investment function where interest rates would be statistically significant and appear with the right sign. All such efforts failed.[7]

The experiences of the economy in 1977–1978 seem to have borne out these apprehensions. From April 1977 to June 1978 the Federal Open Market Committee of the Federal Reserve System tightened credit substantially by raising the federal funds rate that commercial banks charge each other for loans to balance their accounts from 4¾ percent to 7¾ percent—an increase of almost 65 percent—yet the growth rate of the money supply did not slow down. During 1978 the basic money stock (currency and demand deposits) kept rising until October and in the next thirteen weeks declined at a 1.1 percent annual rate, but the velocity, the rate at which the stock of money turns over, increased during the final quarter at an astonishing 9 percent annual rate. The rise in interest rates in that year, reaching a high of 13 percent by the year's end, led many economists to forecast a downturn in construction. Yet this did not happen. One reason may be illustrated by the remark of a builder quoted in the *Wall Street Journal* (January 24, 1979): " 'I don't adjust to interest rates,' says Ray Huffman, a San Diego builder. 'My materials cost 1% more each month. I can't afford to lose rent and lose depreciation by not building. ...' "

The persistence of these attitudes has turned increasing attention to a new, young group of economists who have been building what is called Rational Expectations theory. The premise of the monetarists is that money *counts;* the premise of the new school is that money does not count, because individuals have learned from past experience to *discount* what is happening, and to proceed, on the basis of the information they have, to borrow or not borrow, independent of the momentary monetary rates, in accordance with their judgments of their advantage.

The idea was first put forth by John Muth in 1961 but was elaborated and given powerful technical elaboration by Robert Lucas, of the University of Chicago, in 1972, when he sought to build a notion of stochastic or random shock effects into econometric models, in order to see how such unanticipated effects or reverse movements, particularly in money supply, affected price results in output and employment. Lucas's argument was that such effects are transitory because they are nominal, that money is only a veil in the short run, and that once these shocks are discounted, the classical long-run postulates hold. In effect, Lucas was seeking a way to "discount" the effect of the "discounting" of public decisions by a skeptical public. He was saying that the distrust of governmental measures, fiscal and monetary, was based on a rational calculus of real balances. Through some spectacular mathematical pyrotechnics, a return to the Marshallian notion of equilibrium was being brought about, based on "real" values or, more specifically, on rational expectations.

One can put the problem in simpler, more mundane terms. When the money stock is first increased, people find themselves with more dollars than before and tend to assume that they are wealthier. Businessmen are deceived by distorted price signals, consumers by the number of extra dollars. Thus they act as if this is so, and a rise in output may result. Or, as Lucas puts it: "Everybody thought he was gaining on everybody else. But everybody was wrong. When the true situation becomes clear and real values reassert themselves, people find they have overspent and overborrowed. So when the government tries the same tactic again, the response is far different. When expansionary monetary policy is used repeatedly over time, the kick is lost. There is no stimulating effect on output. Expected expansions come out as inflation and nothing else."

The fact that individuals learn quickly to discount government actions results in an unforeseen collective effect which negates the very intentions the government tries when it tries to alter the economy's course by fiscal or monetary interventions. What, then, should the government do?

The policy argument built around the rational-expectations concept is not that actions of government cannot affect production and employment. They can and do, but only when they surprise people. But to use the old homily, once burnt, twice shy. Or, to use the modern idiom, to get a greater "high," one needs a larger "kick." The crucial point is that government actions which are based on the necessity for surprise can, in the end, only lead to increasing distrust on the part of the polity.

The "rational expectation" view is that some cyclical swings in production and employment are inherent in the *micro* level of the economy which no government *macro* policies can or should attempt to smooth out. This is based on the argument that macro-policy can only deal with aggregates and cannot "fine tune" or choose between the individual decisions of consumers or firms. On the theoretical level, it is based on the assumption that a business cycle is, to some extent, an inextricable aspect of a market economy, because individuals will react differently to price signals, particularly when random shocks (e.g., shortages, sudden price jumps, etc.) lead to a short-term misreading of the signals and to wrong calculations of profit. If misread by enough persons, the changes will create a cumulative swing in output until the misreading is realized, and retrenchment and readjustment set in. Since random shocks to prices and markets are inevitable, because of natural catastrophes or man-made actions, these erratic swings are inevitable. In attempting to meet these, however, the government becomes not the solution but part of the problem, for if the "political discount rate" (i.e., mistrust) is higher than the "economic discount rate" (the nominal expectation of what future costs will be), the actions by government only cause larger and larger perturbations.

It is at this point that Lucas rejoins Friedman on the monetarist conclusions. As regards inflation, monetary authorities should announce, and stick to, a policy that would bring the rate of increase in the general price level to some specified figure, and thereafter monetary policy should seek to reduce uncertainty by maintaining a steady and consistent rate in the growth of the money supply, so that people could build these expectations into their judgments and act accordingly.[8]

The post-Keynesian movement that developed in Anglo-American economics in the 1970s is a complete turn from the monetarist, rational-expectations group and even from the neoclassical school of economics. It rejects general equilibrium theory on the ground that, however elegant, a "timeless" general theory cannot help us understand the variegated changes in modern economic systems. The starting point for the understanding of the economy, the neo-Keynesians assert, is not relative prices which determine distribution but the distribution of income, which determines what will be commanded and produced. The distribution of income is not regarded in the manner of the marginalists, however, for whom each factor in production receives a return proportional to its contribution, but, in the past, as a function of custom, and, in the present, as a consequence of power relations in the market. Inflation is an outcome of the conflict of organized groups for larger shares of the income.

In pure theory, it is a return to the classical economics, as reformulated by Piero Sraffa, with its emphasis on production and the reproduction of the means of production, as the key to the understanding of fundamental economic processes, rather than the subjective utilities of consumer demand. Lionel Robbins had redefined economics as the allocation of scarce resources among competing ends; the neo-Keynesians insist that economics has to deal, first, with growth and investment. On the empirical side, their theory emphasizes institutional relations — the power of organized groups, the character of changes in technology — as the framework of decisions. It differs from orthodox Keynesianism in its emphasis on investment and the long-run processes of the reproduction of the economy, rather than the short-term readjustments (the partial equilibrium of Marshall) of the economy through demand. It differs from Marxist economics in that it eschews the debate over the labor theory of value, the definition of groups in the society necessarily in class terms, and on the idea of the inevitable breakdown of capitalism. It draws much of its inspiration from the group of Cambridge economists who worked with Keynes, such as Sraffa, Joan Robinson, and Nicholas Kaldor, and from economists whose ideas had paralleled Keynes or extended Sraffa, such as Michal Kalecki and Luigi Pasinetti. In the United States a group of younger economists, led by Paul Davidson, Alfred S. Eichner, and J. A. Kregel, have sought to propagate these ideas. They have begun the *Journal of Post-Keynesian Economics,* and a series of essays expounding their point of view appeared in 1978 in the economics magazine *Challenge.*

The starting point for post-Keynesian analysis is the question of growth, or "economic dynamics," as against "economic statics," or the equilibrating mechanisms of an economy with competitive or imperfectly competitive markets. The initial postwar effort to set forth the lineaments of a theory was made by the Oxford economist Roy Harrod (the biographer of Keynes) and formalized by the M.I.T economist Evzey Domar. The Harrod-Domar formula, which they sought to integrate into neoclassical theory, states that the growth rate of an economy (a dependent variable) is determined by the propensity to save (roughly, the rate of savings) and the incremental capital-output ratios, that is, the increases in the productivity of capital. Harrod posited what he called a "warranted" rate of growth—a rate of growth of demand and investment to keep all capital fully utilized—and a "natural" or "potential" rate of growth, which would be sufficient to employ a growing labor force plus any increase in labor productivity. Any shortfalls in these baseline rates would lead to unemployment; any rates that outstripped the growth of capacity and the absorption of a new labor force would create inflation.

A number of technical, empirical, and institutional questions arose over the utility of the Harrod-Domar model, even though it seemed to provide a satisfactory framework for analysis. One was the fact that, as in all such macro-models, capital and labor are considered as aggregates and homogeneous, returns to scale are taken as constant, and consumer tastes and production technologies are considered as unchanged. Yet in any dynamic economy few of these assumptions used in neoclassical theory hold. More to the point: in a dynamic economy, the motor of growth is technology. And how can one "convert" technological change into these standard constants? The problem is how to use such a model, even as a simplified framework, for descriptive analysis or policy decisions.

A different question, raised by the post-Keynesians (in John Cornwall's book *Modern Capitalism*, 1977), was whether a capitalist economy could grow at a rate equal to the warranted and natural rates, thus maintaining full use of capital capacity and full employment.

The crux of the problem is how investment proceeds. In neoclassical theory, savings determine investment, and this is based on the willingness of individuals to forgo current consumption in order to get a satisfactory return (through interest or profit) on their savings. The post-Keynesians believe the reverse: it is investment that determines savings. Based on the work of Kalecki, they argue that investments are financed in large measure out of retained earnings, by profits, and that in oligopolistic situations, firms set their markups sufficiently high so that they can generate sufficient flow from internal sources. (This, for example, is the "standard volume" concept of pricing used by General Motors, as explained by Alfred P. Sloan in his book *My Years With General Motors*.) The empirical issue, then, is the degree of market power of the large corporation to "administer" prices and to adjust production to a set rate of return on investment.

The centrality of investment leads, in post-Keynesian theory, to an argument about distribution, or how incomes are set in the economy. The post-Keynesians reject the view that the income of labor is determined by marginalist principles at the microeconomic level in the labor market. They argue, as did Keynes, that since labor does not know, or cannot choose, the real wage at which it would be employed, nominal wages play the central role in labor's demands. They base a theory of income distribution (derived from essays of Joan Robinson and Nicholas Kaldor, in the *Review of Economic Studies*, 1956) on the argument that an increase in the economic growth rate, because of the higher level of investment, necessarily increases the share of profits in the national income, at the expense of wages.

According to this reasoning, changes in demand, both aggregate and in sectors, are due more to changes in income than to changes in relative prices, and income itself is determined by the market power of contending groups. The rate of inflation is determined, at one end, by the rate of increase of nominal money wages relative to labor productivity—an argument that has recently been reemphasized by Richard Kahn, Keynes's oldest associate at Cambridge, in defending the relevancy of Keynesian theory to the contemporary situation, and in particular to Great Britain. At the other end, it is determined by the ability of large corporations to control the markup of their prices, and even to cut output, rather than price, to maintain their profit ratios. In this analysis, inflation is seen primarily as a cost-push phenomenon: When governmental authorities intervene, particularly through monetary measures, to reduce the money supply, the conflict between the organized groups to safeguard their "market shares" becomes more intense.

The policy prescriptions that follow from such an analysis are an argument for an "incomes policy," a set of wage-and-price controls which would deal not only with aggregate levels but necessarily with the relative wage and price structure between industries and occupations. Basil J. Moore, a post-Keynesian theorist, has written:

> If the government is forced to put itself in the position of regulating wage increases, it will soon be pushed into taking a position not only on appropriate life-cycle income profiles, but also on appropriate relative wage structures among occupations. From there it is but a short step to specifying the appropriate incomes for rentiers and entrepreneurs, and the very foundations of the system will be fundamentally challenged. In order for a modern capitalist system with collective bargaining to avoid stagflation, it becomes necessary to achieve a consensus about equitable relative incomes—and it is precisely this which seems beyond our present political competence.[9]

Most of the orthodox Keynesian economists accept the argument that institutional factors are largely responsible for inflation or instability, without going to the extent of accepting the elaborate theoretical scaffolding of Sraffa or Kalecki. They regard the synthesis of Marshall and Keynes, reformulated by Samuelson and Solow, as a valid model of the economy—*outside* the political system. In the real world, of course, they recognize the crucial role of the political system and seek to produce policy prescriptions through an examination of the interplay of both. But as economists they believe that a pure theory can still be created and serve as a fiction or an "as if"—as if individuals behaved in accordance with the maximizing precepts of rational behavior.

By way of empirical analysis, Charles Schultze, the present chairman of the Council of Economic Advisors, published a monograph in 1959 for the Joint Economic Committee of the Congress, *Recent Inflation in the United States,* which argued that if wages and prices become so sticky that they cannot move downward, inflation is bound to occur. William Nordhaus, a former member of the Council, in an essay on "Inflation Theory and Policy," in the *American Economic Review* of May 1976, posits a "dual economy" model. In one sector there are "auction markets," where supply and demand and flexible prices obtain, as in commodity markets, agricultural products, securities markets, and some internationally traded goods. In the other, there are "administered markets," where the market power of buyers and sellers can limit price movements—in much of manufacturing, utilities, government sectors, and labor markets. The logic of this argument has led economists such as Arthur Okun, Henry Wallich, and Sidney Weintraub to propose that government use tax-incentive policies (TIP) to penalize or reward corporations or firms that set prices or wages beyond a flexible guideline. Yet increasingly, as Edward Tufte and others have pointed out (*Political Control of the Economy,* Princeton University Press, 1978), there is also a "political business cycle," whereby governments, in order to retain popularity, will spend or adjust their budget policies to the timing of elections rather than to the economic business cycle and so create a host of economic problems for the society. As Assar Lindbeck has put it:

> The present 'crisis' in the Western economies is not, I think, mainly a
> 'crisis' in economics, though we economists have no doubt
> overestimated the stability of macroeconometric behavior functions.
> The main problem is not that we are unable to understand analytically
> what is happening, but rather that the institutional changes and the
> discretionary policies that are necessary for macroeconomic stability
> seem to be politically difficult to implement.[10]

And yet—though the subject is far beyond this essay—the fundamental problem may be the very character of economic theory as its major practitioners have fashioned it. Why theory? Because theory directs one to what to see, to the choice of the relevant variables, to the statement as to what is essential about the character of a subject.

Economic theory, by and large, is based on the model of classical mechanics and seeks to create a science in the image of the natural sciences. The model of classical mechanics leads to the idea of an equilibrium, in which natural forces seek to assert themselves and restore economic relations to a balance, the fulcrum of which is perfect competition.* It seeks to be a science by putting its propositions in axiomatic form and setting forth the parameters of different kinds of action so as to create a general, timeless theory and a set of covering laws which would stipulate the range and type of possible actions.

Yet the crucial question is whether economics can be such a science, even within the framework of its self-imposed ordinance of excluding exogenous actions. One can acknowledge, yet put aside, the question of stochastic disturbances, or random shocks, since there may be, as Robert Lucas has attempted to show, ways of building such stochastic disturbances into a model and thus accounting for them. The larger questions are epistemological ones.

Economics deals with "human actions," but it presupposes a definition of rational self-interest as the basis of fictions, or prediction, as if these actions were like laws of physical motion. The result is, basically, a mechanistic view of human behavior. (And Marx, too, in *Kapital,* assumed he could decipher the "laws of motion" of capitalism.) Yet it is not at all clear that this is true, nor, certainly, that prediction is possible—especially if it is based on expectations of human behavior. To put it more formally, as G. L. S. Shackle does in his book *Epistemics & Economics* (Cambridge University Press, 1972), the economic theorist can choose either "rationality" or "time." The theory that rejects time can set forth propositions such as subjective marginalism, and partial or general equilibrium. But the introduction of time not only produces uncertainty but also necessitates understanding the behavior of non-rational actions if it is to deal with the choices human beings make.

One can reformulate the question, as I sought to do several years ago in *The Coming of Post-Industrial Society:*

> The theoretical virtue of the market is that it coordinates human
> interdependence in some optimal fashion, in accordance with the
> expressed preferences of buyers and sellers (within any given
> distribution of income). But what ultimately provides direction for the
> economy, as Veblen pointed out long ago, is not the price system but
> *the value system of the culture* in which the economy is embedded. The
> price system is only a mechanism for the relative allocation of goods
> and services within the framework of *the kinds of demand* generated.
> Accordingly, economic guidance can only be as efficacious as the
> cultural value system which shapes it.[11]

To put the issue in terms of an older philosophical debate, the question is whether economics is *theoretical* or is *practical knowledge,* whether it is a

---

* The idea of treating a social system as a "state of equilibrium" was put forth by Vilfredo Pareto (*The Mind and Society,* p. 66), and through the intermediation of L. J. Henderson, the Harvard physiologist, influenced Talcott Parsons and his work in sociology. But it is no accident, so to speak, that Pareto was initially an economist and an engineer.

natural or a moral science. The predicaments of the last ten or so years and the crisis in economic theory have made that question a central one for the social sciences.

Conventionally, economics is divided into two broad sectors: macro- and microeconomics. Macroeconomics deals with the large magnitudes of gross national product, savings, investment, the money supply, etc. Most of the policy discussions of the economy are within a *macro* framework. Microeconomics is concerned with individual decisions (by persons or firms) in response to prices in markets, on the basis of preferences or wants relative to supply and demand. Macroeconomics, then, is the aggregated behavior of thousands and millions of such individual decisions, as registered by price transactions, and the postulates of microeconomics — the assumptions regarding the behavior of individuals — underlie the conceptual framework of macroeconomic theory.

Neoclassical microeconomic theory is utilitarian. It makes some specific assumptions regarding the actions, if not the motivations, of human beings. What it assumes is that such decisions are rational (i.e., the means chosen seek to fulfill the ends); that they are based on relevant information of alternative prices in markets; and that decisions are made so as to maximize or optimize gains (or efficiency) and to minimize losses (or costs). More formally, these actions can be expressed in "utility preference schedules," or can be "scaled" in a consistent rank order, so that individuals can judge the relative costs or worth of their decisions. Out of these schedules come the more technical tools of economics such as "indifference curves," which means that at roughly equal prices substitutions can take place between different preferences for comparable goods, "production functions," or the different mix of capital or labor at relative prices; or "opportunity costs," meaning that the choice of a resource to one use at an expected gain has to be measured against what may be forgone by an alternative use, etc.

This form of behavior, called "rational action," is usually contrasted with that in a "traditional society," where prices may be set by custom, or factors in production used by habit, or where markets are haphazard or dictated by political rules.

Macroeconomic theory has been challenged in recent years, not only by the argument that the theoretically closed system of interacting variables becomes less meaningful because of the greater role of "exogenous" factors, such as political decisions, but equally by challenges to the postulates of microeconomics itself. Is there such an animal as "economic man," or such conduct as "rational behavior"?

One way of dealing with the question is to say that "rational conduct" is simply a normative standard, an "as if," a theoretical construct of what allocation and distribution would be like *if* people did behave that way; and as a normative standard, it is a measure against which to judge the shortfalls of actual or nonrational conduct. But such an argument eludes the issue by failing to account for the ways individuals actually do behave. Most economists think of their discipline as a positive science, which is both descriptive and explanatory, and they do seek to justify their postulates not just as ideal models but as empirically grounded justifications. They believe man is *Homo economicus* in the arena of production and consumption. It is at this point that the debate in microeconomics in recent years has broken open.

At one end are economists such as Gary Becker of the University of Chicago who argue that not only do individuals act to maximize their gains, that the utilitarian postulates are valid, but that this economic approach can be applied to a wider range of human behavior including areas such as crime or marriage that are usually thought of as noneconomic. For Becker, in fact, economics is not a subject matter, but an approach, an argument that is summed up in his book, *The Economic Approach to Human Behavior* (Chicago: University of Chicago Press, 1976; p. 8). "Indeed," he writes,

> I have come to the position that the economic approach is a
> comprehensive one that is applicable to all human behavior, be it
> behavior involving money prices or imputed shadow prices, repeated
> or infrequent decisions, large or minor decisions, emotional or
> mechanical ends, rich or poor persons, . . . patients or therapists,
> businessmen or politicians, teachers or students. The applications of
> the economic approach so conceived are as extensive as the scope of
> economics in the definition given earlier that emphasizes scarce means
> and competing ends.

Becker and a number of other economists who share this approach argue that maximizing behavior and stable preferences are not simply primitive assumptions but are derivable from the natural selection of adaptive evolutionary behavior, as human beings have evolved over time. These economists have found in sociobiology a support for their arguments. In fact, Jack Hirshleifer, of the University of California of Los Angeles, in an essay "Economics From a Biological Viewpoint," believes that "the fundamental organizing concepts of the dominant analytical structures employed in economics and sociobiology are strikingly parallel."[12]

These versions of "economic man" have been challenged by a number of different social scientists who unite in believing that the postulates of rationality assumed by the utilitarian economists are too abstract and are not demonstrated in actual behavior. One of the earliest and most general challenges was made by Herbert A. Simon, who, though a political scientist and a writer initially on organization behavior, won the Nobel Prize in economics in 1978. In *Administrative Behavior* (3rd ed. 1976), Simon wrote:

> Economic man has a complete and consistent set of preferences that
> allows him always to choose among the alternatives open to him; he is
> always completely aware of what these alternatives are; there are no
> limits on the complexity of the computations he can perform in order

to determine which alternatives are best; probability calculations are neither frightening nor mysterious to him.

But such assumptions of rational choice, argued Simon, have little relation to flesh-and-blood humans. The chief difficulties—and here Simon was drawing on his work in computer science—are the human limits on memory and computing power, and the multiple and conflicting goals in problem-solving.

Against the idea of "economic man," Simon proposed the idea of "bounded rationality." In this he focused on three themes. He proposed that alternatives be discovered through a search in which only a relatively *few* alternatives were considered. Against the scaling of utility preferences in a complete ranked order, he proposed a two-valued utility function, simply satisfactory or unsatisfactory, and subsequent choices followed like branching of a tree from a choice regarding the outcome of the previous decision. In place of the economist's emphasis on choice as a constant set of *new* decisions made for each problem (or in response to price), decisions were seen as a combination of habitual premises and rules that were modified only over the long run.

While these were technical arguments within decision theory, Simon applied them principally to organizational behavior. The notion of "organizational efficiency," derived from "maximizing" or "optimizing" notions, was not applicable to the behavior of organizations. Any organization had conflicting sets of goals; the criteria for success were difficult to agree upon; and most managers rarely acted to maximize their operations, if only because the costs of obtaining all the relevant information were too high or too time-consuming. Instead, what organizations did more typically was to "satisfice"—to follow a course of action that was not necessarily "the best," but good enough to avoid unacceptable levels of trouble. The crucial point was that an organization was not simply an "entrepreneur" but a complex decision-making system of bargains, and one could not understand the behavior of organizations, including economic decisions, without understanding that complexity.[13]

One could argue, in defending the "rational choice" argument, that if an organization itself is a congeries of individuals, each would still seek to maximize his own advantage within the firm, and that while the organization might not be responding fully to the "outside environment" in optimizing its behavior, the decisions might reflect the outcomes and bargains of its major participants. This is the assumption, for example, of J. Kenneth Galbraith in *The New Industrial State* (1967), in which he argues that the "technostructure" or the ruling bureaucracy within the organization acts to safeguard its own interests, as against maximizing the profits of a firm for its shareholders.

But a different argument, within the logic of microeconomic theory itself, is mounted by Harvey Leibenstein of Harvard in his *Beyond Economic Man:*

A New Foundation for Economics (Harvard University Press, 1976). For Leibenstein, cost minimization is the exception rather than the rule in most firms, and in contrast to the idea of *allocative efficiency*, which is used in neoclassical economics, Leibenstein substitutes the terms *X-efficiency* and *X-inefficiency*, i.e., the deviation between the optimal levels of effort from the firm's "rational" viewpoint and the actual levels that individuals achieve. The difference in degree is the "X-efficiency" in the system.

Simply put, Leibenstein argues that in most activities, habit, routine, and entrenched conventions shape the normal course of behavior. For him, the critical measure of efficiency in an organization is the amount and nature of *effort* that an individual makes, and that effort, as such, is not a variable in standard micro theory. In short, for Leibenstein, nonmaximization should be the standard assumption of economic theory, and maximization only a special case. In this emphasis on habit and institution, Leibenstein has gone back to Veblen to recast a theory of microeconomic behavior.

In a very different sense, the postulates of microeconomics have been challenged by Thomas C. Schelling of Harvard in an imaginative book, *Micromotives and Macrobehavior* (New York: Norton, 1978). The basic assumption of economics is that macrobehavior is a *linear* addition of all the individual microdecisions. But for Schelling, what the individual seeks for himself, in the aggregate, often turns into a nightmare. Or, to put it in another way, the "aggregate" is a qualitatively distinct phenomenon from the actions of "individuals."

Schelling draws his models from the commonplaces of everyday life. If a wreck occurs on a highway, cars passing in the opposite lane will slow down to look; all cars in that lane, subsequently, will back up; each car gets a "ten-second" look, yet it costs the entire line ten minutes for that ten-second look. In a gasoline panic, individuals will begin arriving at a gas station at 6:30 A.M. though the station does not open until 7:00. But if each person seeks to arrive even earlier than the other, if enough persons are determined to beat the average, the average itself will get earlier in a "self-displacing prophecy." Each individual is reacting to the expected behavior of the group, but the group is the sum of the individuals. Thus the average arrival time is a "statistical consequence of the behavior [it] induces." Similarly, a tolerant individual may not resent a black family moving into his neighborhood, yet when that number begins to increase, the fear about the fall of property values, induced by the thought that another white neighbor may move, induces the first individual to leave. In short, interacting expectations may be self-fulfilling or self-negating. The same distribution of micromotives can lead to widely divergent macrophenomena, either of greater participation or of withdrawal.

The crucial point is that societal outcomes, when they are the sum total of interacting individuals, often lead to outcomes which none of the individuals desires. The well-known illustration is Garrett Hardin's example of the "tragedy of the commons" (*Science,* Dec. 13, 1968, pp. 1243–48), where a shared resource, a grazing area, is used by each individual for his own maximizing advantage until in the end the resource is destroyed. If a single individual withholds his cows to preserve the grass, he gains no advantage, but the others do. Conversely, in other situations where goods are public or collective (e.g., a trade-union collective-bargaining contract), an individual who does not pay for the outcome may yet receive it and become a free rider. In short, since interacting individuals, acting only on "micromotives," are unlikely to coordinate their activities, some group or collective action is needed. Schelling concludes:

> A good part of social organization consists of institutional arrangements to overcome these divergences between perceived individual interest and some larger collective bargain. [The collective bargain above is for everyone to graze fewer cows so the pasture survives.] Some of it is market-oriented—ownership, contracts ... and a variety of communications and information systems. Some have to do with government—taxes to cover public services.... More selective groupings—the union, the club, the neighborhood—can organize incentive systems or regulations to try to help people do what individually they wouldn't but collectively they may wish to do. Our morals can substitute for markets and regulations in getting us sometimes to do from conscience the things that in the long run we might elect to do only if assured of reciprocation [pp. 127–28].

In sum, if economic activities are social processes, can one have an adequate theory of economic behavior outside the framework of a comprehensive sociological theory? It is a question that economists and sociologists will be pursuing in the next decade.

3. Neo-Marxism

In the 1960s and 1970s, one saw a surprising upsurge of Marxist politics and neo-Marxist thought on a scale largely unexpected, following the sense of an exhaustion of radical ideas in the West by the end of the 1950s.* Three developments may have accounted for this change.

---

* Since I am prominently identified with the theme of the "end of ideology," which received considerable attention in the early 1960s, it is not amiss to point out that many persons have read the argument from the title of my book, not from its contents.

The book dealt with the "exhaustion of political ideas in the Fifties," which is the subtitle of the book, and states two propositions: One, that a "new generation, with no meaningful memory of these old debates and no secure tradition to build upon" is searching yearningly and desperately for "a cause" to build new faiths. And two, "that while the old nineteenth-century ideologies and intellectual debates have become exhausted, the rising states of Africa and Asia are fashioning new ideologies with a different appeal for their own people.... The ideologies of the nineteenth century were universalistic, humanistic, and fashioned by intellectuals. The mass ideologies of Asia and Africa are parochial, instrumental, and created by political leaders." See *The End of Ideology* (Glencoe, Ill.: The Free Press, 1960, rev. ed. 1962), pp. 40, 373.

One was the emergence of a large number of third-world countries such as Cuba, Vietnam, Cambodia, Mozambique, and Angola, which called themselves Marxist, and an array of other countries, as diverse as Southern Yemen, Afghanistan, Libya, or Algeria, which called themselves in one form or another socialist. The paradox is that little of this emerged out of classical Marxist theory, which, in its Western evolutionary framework, saw socialism as the next, higher stage after capitalism. These were almost all former colonial peasant societies which had come under the leadership of young elites that were seeking to transform them from the top, through state direction. Their leaders, like Calibans, had learned a language and used it to curse. Their Marxism was a rhetoric of anti-imperialism and a technique for political mobilization.

A second reason was the youth upsurge in the 1960s, in the Western industrial countries, against Establishment and Authority. There was an emphasis on spontaneity and "doing one's thing," on participation, on communitarianism, and an attack on materialism and consumerism. Its root impulse, thematically, was on the grosser features of capitalist society, and its initial impacts were in culture (or, more specially the "counterculture") and on the quality-of-life issues in politics, particularly ecology and the environment. Sometimes parallel and sometimes intertwined were the drive of the blacks for civil rights and the demand by women for equal rights. Intellectually inchoate and populist in temper, as the young radicals of the 1960s began to move into the institutions, particularly the universities, and as the recession of the 1970s seemed to herald the economic decline of the Western countries, many of the younger scholars turned to various forms of neo-Marxism to refine their ideas and to explore a more coherent kind of social analysis.

The third reason, somewhat independent at first, yet finally providing a new foundation, was the independent scholarship in Marxist studies that had begun to emerge in the 1950s and the publication of many of the texts of Marx that had been suppressed or ignored by the predominant Communist monopoly in the publication of Marx's works during the years following the Russian Revolution. The "rediscovery" of forgotten Marxist writers of the 1920s, such as Lukács, Gramsci, and Korsch, or the sudden emergence of the "Frankfurt School," including Horkheimer, Adorno, Marcuse (and as a younger follower Jürgen Habermas), all provided the basis for a tremendous industry of publication of older texts, intense discussion of their ideas, and tremendous outpouring of exegetical arguments as to what Marx really meant, or the relevance of Marx to the day.

It would take an essay as long as these two parts combined merely to sketch the diverse issues and the many revisionist quarrels in a dozen different fields which this new burst of intellectual energy produced. In any philosophical world view grounded in a faith system, such as Christianity, the minute dissection of "the Word" assumes a fateful character. As in

Christianity, where if the wrong *letter* is employed (*homoiousian* as against *homoousian*) one risks loss of salvation, so, in Marxism, the slightest doctrinal deviation risks derailing the Revolution from the track of History.

And the difficulty of Marxism was—and is—that definitive texts are lacking. Even today there is no complete set of all the writings of Marx and Engels. And when they are completed, the problems will not change because of the contradictory dilemmas that Marx faced in wrestling with crucial philosophical issues: the questions of voluntarism (in which men make their own history) versus determinism; an activity theory of knowledge versus a copy theory of knowledge; human nature as possessing an essence (*Wesen*) or a human nature that changes as a consequence of the growth of men's technical powers.[14]

The striking thing is that few if any of the early philosophical works of Marx—*The German Ideology* and the *Economic-Philosophical Manuscripts*, written before 1847, and the sketchy but massive sociological treatise, the so-called *Grundrisse*, or Outlines of National Economy (1857–59)—not only were not published in Marx's lifetime but did not even appear until a half-century after his death—the first two in the 1930s in German (and much later in English) and the last in the 1950s in German. Marx completed only the first volume of *Das Kapital;* the other two volumes were arbitrarily organized by Engels, while a large sheaf of auxiliary materials, the *Theorien über den Mehrwert* (Theories of Surplus Value), were published in four volumes only after the death of Engels by his literary executor, Karl Kautsky, and still remain incompletely translated into English. Even the early English translations of many of Marx's works, including *Kapital*, are clumsy and inexact and only now are being redone.

The first generation of Marxian theoreticians, among them Kautsky, Lenin, and Plekhanov, knew little if any of the early works. Their conceptions of Marxism derived from the first codification of Marx's work, the book by Frederick Engels, *Anti-Dühring*, and from the pamphlet derived from it, *Socialism, Utopian and Scientific*. Engels was largely dismissive of the early works, and when asked by a visitor in 1893 why he did not publish them, Engels remarked that one needed a knowledge of Hegel to understand them, that many were now obscure in their metaphysical jargon, and that his important task was to complete the publication of *Kapital*, which he regarded as the major achievement of Marx.

Regarding the early philosophical works: in 1876 Engels wrote a long review essay of a book by a man named Starcke, on Feuerbach, Marx's immediate intellectual mentor, which he published as *Ludwig Feuerbach and the Outcome of Classical German Philosophy*. To this he appended the fragmentary and incomplete (they are little more than gnomic jottings) paragraphs of Marx called the "Theses on Feuerbach," which Engels regarded as the most "meaty" of those older philosophical statements.

One curious result is that concepts which, in the past twenty years, have seemed to be inextricably associated with the name of Marx were almost completely unknown and never appeared in the writings of the first generation of Marx's expositors. The most striking is the concept of *alienation*. The term does not appear in any of the writings of Engels, Plekhanov, Kautsky, or Lenin. The entry on "alienation" in the authoritative *Encyclopaedia of the Social Sciences* (1931) deals only with "alienation of property," as a legal term, while the biographical entry on Marx (1933), by Karl Korsch, a major Marxist philosopher, does not mention the term. The magisterial study by Sidney Hook, *From Hegel to Marx* (1936), a meticulous study of the development of Marx's thought from Hegel through the various left-Hegelian writers to Marx, carries only a passing reference to the term, and the word itself, *alienation*, does not appear in the index of the book.

Yet in the major writings on Marx in the 1960s and after, the term *alienation* is regarded as the central concept in Marx's thought. The major work by the French Catholic writer, Père Jean-Yves Calvez, *La Pensée de Karl Marx*, is a 600-page book in which it is used as the organizing theme to explore all of Marx's work. This is equally true of the work of Iring Fetscher, the German scholar. And the theme has been used by more popular if less exacting writers such as Bertell Ollmann and Richard Schacht.

All this has given rise to an exegetical debate as to whether there was a *continuity* in Marx's thought, or a rupture. David McClellan, a prolific writer on the subject and a recent biographer of Marx, argues that there is a consistency and continuity to Marx's thought, especially, he points out, as the term *alienation* is used in the *Grundrisse*. Writers as diverse as Sidney Hook and Louis Althusser argue, for different intellectual reasons, that there was a "break" in Marx's writings, though each dates it differently. For Hook, the term *alienation* was a product of German romanticism, which Marx himself later mocked, and had disappeared because Marx, beginning with *The German Ideology*, sought to locate social relations in more exact class terms. For Althusser, the decisive break comes with the writing of *Kapital*, which he regards as the basis of Marx's "scientific" work, as against philosophy. For an outsider, these may seem puzzling and only doctrinal quarrels, yet to the extent that doctrine shapes or justifies large intellectual structures, let alone political movements, in the beginning—and in the end—is the Word.

The difficulty with all this is compounded by the fact that on *any* single major concept associated with the name of Marx there is no single unambiguous definition of the terms involved. The phrase *historical materialism* was never used by Marx but was coined by Engels. The term *dialectical materialism* was never used by either Marx or Engels but was created by the Russian Marxist Plekhanov.

Let us take a key idea. Marxist sociology can probably be summed up in a single sentence: "All social structure is, fundamentally, class structure." That is Marxism's strength; it is also its problem. To say that all social divisions in society are derived from class is to give one a powerful prism on social behavior. It posits a single axis that divides basic interests; it identifies different world views (even truths) and different life-styles in class terms. The difficulty is that the statement is more metaphoric than denotative. It begins to founder when one asks: what does one mean by class?

Marx, in fact, uses the term *class* in five different ways. Even when, most broadly, class is related primarily to the structure of production, as the essential classes (i.e., the large bulk of tradesmen, professionals, priests, officers, and government employees are placed outside the productive process and supported by the "value" produced by the workers), the boundary definitions are vague. Who belongs to the working class? Is it only production or factory workers? Where does one fit in clerical and technical personnel? What of managers who are salaried individuals yet run the enterprises? Who are "the capitalists"? What does it mean to "own" property? Who owns the mutual insurance companies that possess the largest aggregate of disposable capital in the United States? And who "owns" A.T.&T. or Exxon or General Motors, the largest capitalist corporations in the country?

No wonder that even committed Marxists are baffled. The exploration and reinterpretation of Marx have gone into every field — philosophy, aesthetics, history, sociology, and economics. One should distinguish, again, the political and moral criticism of capitalism from a radical standpoint (and the validity this might have) from the effort to ground a new philosophy and social science out of the thought of Marx. It is these latter efforts that will be touched upon, if necessarily briefly.

The major starting point has been philosophy. Here, what has been termed "classical Marxism" has been the subject of the most heated debate and thoroughgoing revision. Classical Marxism, as put forth by Engels, emphasized a "copy theory of knowledge," i.e., that what we know is a reflection of the external reality. This, of course, was a mechanistic position, since materialism was the foundation of knowledge, and to show change, even in nature, it was held that "matter" moved "dialectically." Engels also sought to cast Marxism in a "scientific" vein, according to the mode of the time, by emphasizing determinism and "laws" of society almost on the model of physics — an effort that found its doctrinal support in Marx's brief methodological assertions in the Author's Prefaces to *Kapital* that he was not describing capitalism empirically but as abstractions are used in the physical sciences, and that he was seeking to identify the "laws of motion" of capitalism.

Yet, as George Lichtheim, one of the early independent scholars of the subject, pointed out in his *Marxism: An Historical and Critical Study* (London: Routledge & Kegan Paul, 1961), this "scientistic" view clashed with the early writings of Marx, which contained an "activity theory of knowledge" that was rooted in the development of consciousness.

What Lichtheim was summing up was a view, expressed in more technical ways, that Marx's ideas were directly rooted in Hegel, and that this had radically different consequences for understanding Marx than the deterministic reading by Engels. The question whether Engels had radically revised Marx, or whether Marx himself had surrendered some of his early views, bedevils Marxist debates today.

Marxist philosophy in the last decade and a half has centered on the thoughts of four views: that of György Lukács, the Hungarian philospher; the "Frankfurt School," which includes Max Horkheimer, Theodor Adorno, Herbert Marcuse, and, as a later votary, Jürgen Habermas; Jean-Paul Sartre, the French existentialist who sought to graft Marxist thought onto his earlier writing; and the French philosopher Louis Althusser.

Lukács, who has been the most influential (and enigmatic) Marxian critic, had in 1923 published a book entitled *History and Class Consciousness* in which, without knowing directly of the early writing of Marx, he "intuited" on the basis of his reading of Hegel a different view of Marx from the orthodox view prevailing at the time. But Lukács, in 1923 and later in 1930, was forced, ignominiously, to recant the book and, as a devoted Communist, he forbade any reprint of it. For many years it led a subterranean existence as an esoteric text, in part because of its "gnostic" inference that the intellectuals were the true, inner elite of the vanguard, a theme that Thomas Mann depicted in his portrait of Lukács as Naphta, the Jesuit revolutionist, in *The Magic Mountain*. Lukács derided dialectical materialism as simply "inverted Platonism," without any philosophical foundation, but he also gave a radical interpretation to the theory of historical materialism. For Lukács, there was no "independent" view of reality and history outside of "class views," and knowledge, therefore, was always class-bound. But if this was the case, which view was "true"? For Lukács, the view of the proletariat was true—even if the proletariat itself did not hold that view—because in the immanent development of consciousness, the proletariat was the "human subject" that alone could achieve universality, the consideration of reason, this being, for Lukács, something historical.

The question whether there is a *marche générale*, of History, and more, whether Stalinism, despite its "excesses," was "historically progressive," was the inner debate that wracked the Commmunist intelligentsia. If morality is only class morality, from what standpoint could one condemn the forced collectivization and the concentration camps? How does one know in which direction History is marching and whether "the Party," as embodied in the current leader, is on the course dictated by the "cunning reason"? Lukács himself was always ambiguous, publicly, about Stalinism. Though he became a minister in the short-lived cabinet of Imre Nagy, during the Hungarian Revolution of 1956, and was arrested and deported when the Russian troops crushed the dissident Communist rebellion (Nagy himself was shot), Lukács never wavered in his support of the ultimately "progressive" role of the Russian Revolution.

The Frankfurt School was never communist—Adorno once said of Lukács that "[He] tugs vainly at his chains and imagines their clanking to be the forward march of *der Weltgeist*" (the world-spirit), though Marcuse, in his book *Soviet Marxism*, was more ambiguous regarding the "historical" role of the Russian Revolution.

The Frankfurt School, founded originally at that university, saw as its main task the development of "critical theory." By this it meant an attack on positivism, and the development of a "negative dialectic," i.e., the exposure of the retrograde features of "bourgeois" Enlightenment philosophy, such as its emphasis on egoism and individualism, the uncritical view of "progress," and, in particular, the role of "technological rationality" as the basis of functional efficiency. The attacks on technology and on mass culture were the central themes of Marcuse, particularly in *One-Dimensional Man*, and of Adorno in collections of essays, such as *Prisms*. Positivism was seen as the acceptance of existing empirical reality as truth.

If one asks from what standpoint it is that one makes the criticisms, the answers become more uncertain. Formally it was the idea of Reason, expressed in different ways. For Adorno, it was the idea of "authenticity"; for Marcuse, as in his book *Eros and Civilization*, it is the lifting of all "repression" so that libidinal energies are freed for creative tasks; for Jürgen Habermas, who has attempted the most thoroughgoing critique of contemporary philosophy (in his *Knowledge and Human Interests*), it is the effort to achieve "undistorted communication." Where for Francis Bacon, in his *Novum Organum*, men were divided by the "idols of the tribe," the "idols of the market," and so forth, for Habermas it is no longer the direct exploitation of the worker by the capitalist that inhibits the rational development of the productive capacity of the society but the nature of science and technology itself. As he writes in his book *Toward a Rational Society:*

> ... technology and science become a leading productive force,
> rendering inoperative the conditions for Marx's labor theory of value.
> It is no longer meaningful to calculate the amount of capital
> investment in research and development on the basis of the value of
> unskilled (simple) labor power, when scientific-technical progress has
> become an independent source of surplus value, in relation to which
> the only source of surplus value considered by Marx, namely the labor
> power of the immediate producers, plays an ever smaller role.[15]

The "critique" of science in its various positivist guises becomes, then, one of the main tasks of philosophy. The positive goal, however, is to achieve "inter-subjectivity," or common understandings among men, and only when all ideological and communication "distortions" are eliminated can men begin to define their "knowledge-constitutive interests," those which give them true insight into their authentic needs.

For Sartre, too, in his *Critique de la raison dialectique*, the problem of "standpoint" is crucial. Sartre, too, reasserts the Hegelian principle that History unfolds the truth about man, and he rejects the "copy theory of knowledge" of Engels—and of Lenin, who followed this in his *Materialism and Empirio-*

Criticism. The first limitation of Marxism, argues Sartre, is its failure to put forth a theory of "mediation," or how one moves from the abstract "concepts" about nature and history to the concrete lives of individuals and the specificity of events—the themes that existentialism had taken as primary. Marxism, argues Sartre, has failed because it subordinates individuals to a preconceived schematism. The second limitation is the materialist dialectic, which roots the historical process in nature, where, for Sartre, the ontological vantage point is the dialectical movement of men to freedom. What inhibits freedom, says Sartre, is scarcity, which, in a theme going back to Hobbes, forces men to treat each other as instruments or things, or as "others." The dialectic of history is *altérité* (otherness), and *alienation* as created by scarcity. Since these divide men, the standpoint of judgment, of emancipation, is that which creates "wholeness" or the ensembles of totality in human relations.

The major thrust of almost all neo-Marxian philosophy was to return to Hegel, and to the historicism that is at its core. But Hegel's historicism presents three problems: it sees the world in dualistic terms, e.g., subject and object, spirit and matter, nature and history, etc.; it posits an immanent process of unfolding in which these dualities become resolved at "higher" levels of unity; and it holds, necessarily, that man has no nature but a history. But if so, what is the thread of understanding from the past to the present? In a simple sense, if human nature today, because of greater consciousness or technical powers, differs from that of ancient Greece, how do "we" understand one another? For Hegel, as for Marx, Greek art represented the "childhood" of the human race.

In his early writings, Marx had sought to *overcome* philosophy by the revolutionary union of theory and practice (e.g., the theses on Feuerbach), but the "later" Marx, or Engels, rejected this dualism by investing his faith in science—though, as George Lichtheim remarks, "he left it to Engels to complete the circle with the construction of a materialist ontology which reads the dialectic back into nature."[16]

What Louis Althusser, the French communist philosopher, has sought to do is to repudiate the Hegelian and historicist interpretations of Marx and to restore the "scientific" method which he believes Marx created in *Kapital*. For Althusser, the early writings represent a "humanist" Marx who simply becomes entangled with the problems of subjectivity. What he proposes as distinctive about Marx is the emphasis on the structure of relations, the *Darstellung*, as the independent object of study within the mode of production. In short, à la mode, what Althusser has given us is a "structuralist Marx" to replace the Hegelian Marx. It is a topic to which we shall revert in the next major section, on structuralism.

Marxian social theory has had three components. One, rooted in the early philosophical writings, is the idea that socialism is the fulfillment of the Enlightenment, the overcoming of all dualities (in philosophy, of subject and object, spirit and matter; in the social world, of mental and physical labor, town and country labor), the "realization" of History in the universalization of human society. As Marx remarked, in his essays on *The Jewish Question,* bourgeois society had brought political emancipation in the freedom of property and the freedom of religion, whereas socialism would mean human emancipation, or the freedom from property and the freedom from religion. Man's command over nature would be matched by his command of his own fate.

The second component of traditional Marxism, beginning with the *Poverty of Philosophy* and extending through *Kapital,* is a structural analysis of capitalism as an integral system of commodity production, which, because of competition and the changing organic composition of capital (i.e., the shrinking base of labor), must come into crisis and eventually give way, owing to the social character of production, to socialism.

The third component, which found its most mechanistic exposition in Engels, is a general theory of society in which all social structure is conceptualized on the basis of a substructure and superstructure; in which the mode of production is seen as determining all other social relations; and in which class positions within the mode of production (read back into history, as well) become the basis of the polarization of society.

Of these three components, the first derived from an evolutionary Hegelian vision which saw increasing rationality and the growth of self-consciousness as the motor forces of history. While the normative views of socialism from this vision may remain as utopia, as history or philosophy they are patently deficient.

The second view surely had great analytical power in dealing with capitalism from 1750 to 1950, but it is questionable whether the actual theoretical formulations remain valid in the state-directed and post-industrial worlds of the latter part of the twentieth century. Capitalism as a socioeconomic system may decline, but it is questionable whether it will do so for the reasons that Marx, rather than, say, Schumpeter (in his *Capitalism, Socialism, and Democracy*), adduced.

As to the "general theory of society," the mechanistic and positivist formulations going back to Engels have increasingly been abandoned; the inadequacy of reading pre-capitalist and certainly non-Western societies in class terms has been recognized; and the fumbling efforts to redefine mode of production as crossed by "social formations" all attest a dissolution of what had once been, at least, a straightforward determinist theory of society.

What is most striking, perhaps, has been the inadequacy of Marxist theory to explain "Marxist" societies. By what Marxist categories does one explain the deep tensions between the Soviet Union and China, or the violent, eruptive outbreak of hostilities between Vietnam and Cambodia? If one takes the Soviet Union as a society that has existed now for more than sixty years, how does one explain the new class structure of that society with the growth of new, privileged strata? In 1957 Milovan Djilas, the former Yugoslav communist leader, wrote *The New Class*, in which he argued that the bureaucracy in the Soviet Union had become the basis of a new class system; but Marxism has never had an adequate theory of the nature of bureaucracy. Lenin, in *State and Revolution*, argued that under socialism, administrative tasks would be so simplified that any person could take his turn in the administration of the State. Max Weber, writing at the same time but more presciently, argued in *Economy and Society* that socialism would become even more bureaucratic than capitalism because of the technical nature of administration and the requirements of planning. More recently, two Hungarian sociologists, György Konrád and Iván Szelényi, based on their experiences in Hungary, published a book, *The Intellectuals on the Road to Class Power: A Sociological Study of the Role of the Intelligentsia in Socialism* (New York: Harcourt Brace Jovanovich, 1979), which argues that the intelligentsia has become a new class, but one that invariably comes into conflict with the political party elite. From the Soviet Union through Yugoslavia to Cuba, what the various studies of different Communist societies fail to explore is the *rebirth* of inequality after the revolutions and the institutionalization of that inequality into new systems of privilege. A primitive explanation goes back to functionalist theory, e.g., that the "time" of a manager is worth more than that of a worker, since he has greater responsibilities for coordination, and that greater privileges such as an automobile and chauffeur need to be provided for him than for the worker. That may explain the inequality of *functional position*, but not necessarily why the advantages to the individuals in those positions are passed on to their children. A more promising explanation is that, though private property has been eliminated as a source of privilege in "socialist" societies, given the technical nature of the societies, skill, or "intellectual capital," or "cultural capital," becomes the main source of differentiation, and its advantages are passed on differentially to the children in the society. In effect, there is (as Bakunin and Machakski argued long ago) a "functional" reason why the intelligentsia are the inevitable privileged class under socialism; and this gives some pith to the gnomic remark of Alvin Gouldner, in his book *The Future of Intellectuals and the Rise of the New Class* (1979), that "Marxism is the false consciousness of the intelligentsia."

While no final word can ever be said on a doctrine as protean as Marxism, one should call attention to the three-volume work by Leszek Kołakowski, *Main Currents of Marxism: Its Rise, Growth, and Disillusion* (Oxford: The Clarendon Press, 1978). Kołakowski was in the late 1950s the most brilliant Marxist philosopher in Poland, one of the organizers of the paper *Po Prostu* that inspired the Polish upheavals in 1956, and, until 1968, when expelled from the post, he was Professor of the History of Philosophy at the University of Warsaw. Since then he has been, principally, a Fellow of All Souls College,

Oxford. The *Main Currents* is his major, synoptic effort to treat Marxism as the history of a doctrine. The first volume deals with the "Founders," the second, the "Golden Age," with the first generation of exegetes, and the third, the "Breakdown," with both Stalinism and the major neo-Marxist philosophers such as Lukács, Gramsci, Marcuse, and others. There is no single thread which runs through the 1,500 pages of detailed exposition and philosophical glosses; it is a patient effort to sort out the variety of conflicting formulations and judgments. Yet in the Epilogue Kołakowski, who had been hailed twenty-five years ago as the most brilliant Marxist philosopher of his generation, permits himself some personal reflections. He writes:

> Marxism has been the greatest fantasy of our century. It was a dream offering the prospect of a society of perfect unity, in which all human aspirations would be fulfilled and all values reconciled. . . .
>
> To say that Marxism is a fantasy does not mean that it is nothing else. Marxism as an interpretation of past history must be distinguished from Marxism as a political ideology. No reasonable person would deny that the doctrine of historical materialism has been a valuable addition to our intellectual equipment and has enriched our understanding of the past. True, it has been argued that in a strict form the doctrine is nonsense and in a loose form it is a commonplace; but, if it has become a commonplace, this is largely thanks to Marx's originality. Moreover, if Marxism has led towards a better understanding of the economics and civilization of past ages, this is no doubt connected with the fact that Marx at times enunciated his theory in extreme, dogmatic, and unacceptable forms. If his views had been hedged round with all the restrictions and reservations that are usual in a rational thought, they would have had less influence and might have gone unnoticed altogether. As it was, and as often happens with humanistic theories, the element of absurdity was effective in transmitting their rational content. . . .
>
> As an explanatory 'system' it is dead, nor does it offer any 'method' that can be effectively used to interpret modern life, to foresee the future, or cultivate utopian projections. Contemporary Marxist literature, although plentiful in quantity, has a depressing air of sterility and helplessness, in so far as it is not purely historical. . . .
>
> The influence that Marxism has achieved, far from being the result or proof of its scientific character, is almost entirely due to its prophetic, fantastic, and irrational elements. Marxism is a doctrine of blind confidence that a paradise of universal satisfaction is awaiting us just round the corner. Almost all the prophecies of Marx and his followers have already proved to be false, but this does not disturb the spiritual certainty of the faithful, any more than it did in the case of chiliastic sects: for it is a certainty not based on any empirical premises or supposed 'historical laws', but simply on the psychological need for certainty. In this sense Marxism performs the function of a religion,

and its efficacy is of a religious character. But it is a caricature and a bogus form of religion, since it presents its temporal eschatology as a scientific system, which religious mythologies do not purport to be.

4. Structuralism

In a UNESCO volume published ten years ago, intended to sum up the state of our knowledge in the "social and human sciences," the noted Swiss psychologist Jean Piaget wrote:

> One of the most general trends of avant-garde movements in all the human sciences is structuralism, which is taking the place of atomistic attitudes or 'holistic' explanations (emergent wholes).[17]

What may have been an avant-garde movement ten years ago is today a flood tide. Structuralism seems to have swept through almost every area of literary and social-science studies, producing a huge literature in which the names of Piaget in psychology, Claude Lévi-Strauss in anthropology, Jacques Lacan in psychoanalysis, Louis Althusser in Marxist studies, Michel Foucault in epistemology and the history of ideas, and Jacques Derrida and Roland Barthes in literature are especially distinguished. Looming in the background are the works of Ferdinand de Saussure and Roman Jakobson and the revolution in linguistics associated with their names, a revolution whose ideas about the nature of language and the system of signs undergird almost all the diverse work in the various disciplines that have been called structuralist. Yet among these writers, as among those who seek to expound or popularize their doctrines, one finds almost no agreement as to what structuralism *is*. "What is structuralism," writes Roland Barthes:

> It is not a school of thought, or even a movement, for most of the authors habitually associated with this word do not feel in any way bound together by a common doctrine or cause. It is hardly a well-defined term: *structure* is a word of long standing (derived from anatomy and grammar) which today suffers from excessive use.*

And if one turns to the highly lucid work by Howard Gardner, *The Quest for Mind: Piaget, Lévi-Strauss and the Structuralist Movement*, one finds Gardner disclaiming definition at the start:

> The fact is, I think, that it is not possible to define the movement with any precision, any more than it is to delineate clearly a field called social psychology or behavioral genetics. Writers have tended to apply the term 'structuralism' either to a hopelessly vague field of literary analysis, to all contemporary French intellectual thought which is not

---

* Quoted in Jean-Marie Benoist, *The Structural Revolution*, (London: Weidenfeld and Nicolson, 1978), p. 1.

avowedly existentialist, or to the writings of any and all scholars and critics who call themselves structuralists. Certainly none of these approaches is wholly satisfactory. Add to the confusion that no two structuralists, not even Lévi-Strauss and Piaget, define 'structure' in the same way, and one wonders why the term has not been publicly banned or appropriated by Newspeak.[18]

Gardner may have spoken from hindsight, for in looking at a trendy anthology entitled *The Structuralists from Marx to Lévi-Strauss*, one might say that Newspeak had been quick to seize the day. The editors, Richard T. and Fernande M. De George, open their introduction by remarking:

> Structuralism has been described as a method, a movement, an intellectual fad, and an ideology. Each of these characterizations is in part valid. For structuralism is a loose, amorphous, many-faceted phenomenon with no clear lines of demarcation, no tightly knit group spearheading it, no specific set of doctrines held by all those whom one usually thinks of as being associated with it. It cuts across many disciplines—linguistics, anthropology, literary criticism, psychology, philosophy. For some it gives hope of uncovering or developing a common basic approach to the social sciences, literature and art which would unify them and put them on a scientific footing, much as the 'scientific method' grounds and unifies the physical sciences.*

After which these editors proceed to locate the roots of structuralism in the nineteenth century in the thought of Marx, Freud, and de Saussure:

> What Marx, Freud and Saussure have in common, and what they share with present day structuralists, is a conviction that surface events and phenomena are to be explained by structures, data and phenomena below the surface. The explicit and the obvious is to be explained by and is determined—in some sense of the term—by what is implicit and not obvious. The attempt to uncover deep structures, unconscious motivations, and underlying causes which account for human actions at a more basic and profound level than do individual conscious decisions, and which shape, influence and structure these decisions, is an enterprise which unites Marx, Freud, Saussure, and modern structuralists.[19]

Unhappily, such claims dissolve any distinctive meaning to structuralism, for the idea of an underlying structure—the distinction between appearance and reality—is co-extensive with the entire history of Western philosophy, especially gnosticism and mysticism. In the pre-Socratics, beginning with Thales, we have the effort to find an underlying substance to the diversity of elements, and these were variously located as air, earth, water, or fire; and with these were associated the qualities of wet, dry, hot, or cold,

---

* An unfortunate figure of speech, since the avant-garde movement in the philosophy of science, from Paul Feyerabend to Stephen Toulmin, denies the distinctiveness of something called "the scientific method."

so the cross-classification of elements and properties (e.g., fire is hot and dry, etc.) gave one a substructure to the physical world. Plato's divided line distinguished between the visible (sensory) and the intelligible (conceptual) and saw knowledge as a movement from the one to the other. Aristotle saw the hidden design of any object in its "entelechy," the movement to the realization of its immanent form; this biological theme was later recast by Hegel and Marx in the idea of "necessity" as the realization of History. And for Kant, the categories of understanding—basically space and time, which were the intrinsic properties of mind—organized the flux of experience into intelligible concepts.

If one seeks to understand the distinctiveness of structuralism, one has to see it as a movement with a specific *epistemological* program, no matter how diverse its various applications. One can, perhaps, identify six elements of this program.

1. *The search for invariant relations on the model of the natural sciences.* The starting point here is Galileo. In reacting against the "essentialism" of Aristotle, who looked for the qualitative differences between phenomena and classified these as *types*, Galileo introduced the idea of a field. Specifically, Galileo did not study "concrete" objects but their abstract properties, not a falling body but attributes such as mass, acceleration, velocity, and the like, and he sought to find the quantitative relations between these properties which would govern any specific body. Structuralism makes no distinction between the natural and human sciences and, as we shall see, claims to find isomorphic structures between physical and psychological phenomena.

2. *Against historicism, or "diachronic" analysis,* structuralism rejects the idea that a phenomenon is to be understood through its genesis. In one variant it sees "history" as contingent and variable and therefore without a distinct pattern; in another version, as too deterministic, like a Hegelian scheme. (For Hegel, only the West had a history, for only the West had a "rational" development and was not bound to nature; all other social forms were "frozen.") Structuralism rejects the idea that the character of a phenomenon is to be understood as derived from its historical context.

3. *Against subjectivity.* Classical philosophy had no concept of a theory of the "knowing subject," an individual who is the judge of knowledge. Plato, indeed, denied the idea of such an individual. Knowledge was located in the "predicates," the ideal forms under which particulars were subsumed. With Descartes we find the problem of the "knower" replacing that of the "known" as the problem for philosophy, a dualism of mind and body, and an implicit relativism in which the vantage point of the knower becomes the starting point of inquiry. With subjectivity we also find a radical humanism, as in existentialism, in which the individual person, his free will and his responsibility, becomes the source of truth—for him or her.

Structuralism seeks to replace the human subject—the individual or the thinking consciousness, the transcendental ego—as the unit of study with the *relations* between individuals, the products and objects of the interactions, and the linguistic code and invariant structures as the knowledge which has intelligibility. One can say that it is the supremacy of the code over that which is codified (the content), the synchronic over the diachronic, the model over the diverse facts.

4. *The congruence of a linguistic structure as the embodiment of the modes of thought and the relational rules derived from them with all other modes of cultural or social relations.* Common to almost all structuralism is the idea, derived from de Saussure, that language is an ordered system of signs, a distinct system with its own rules and properties that can be stated without reference to historical or extra-linguistic factors, like the rules of chess that govern the system of play. With this in mind, Lévi-Strauss argues that all cultural phenomena should be considered in terms of signs. And, indeed, for him society is interpretable as an "ensemble" of three different kinds of communication — the exchange of messages, the exchange of commodities (i.e., goods and services), and the exchange of women (i.e., marriage and kinship rules) — each of which is distinct, but all together make a common structural field. Within this view, social anthropology, economics, and linguistics are all subsumed under the common rubric of the semiotic.

5. *The argument, though more true of Lévi-Strauss and Piaget (and, in a different context, of Noam Chomsky), that the underlying structure of mind is rational.*

In the history of ideas, this has two radical consequences. One is to abolish the distinction between the savage and the modern as two different types of thought, the one ruled by magic and the other by science, or, in the older distinction of Lévy-Bruhl, between the pre-logical and logical. For Lévi-Strauss, the savage mind is as logical as the modern, but in its own mode. For example, in his study of *Totemism* (Boston: Beacon Press, 1963), Lévi-Strauss insisted that the totem of a clan was not a magical or animistic symbol for some abstract taboo, but a means of enforcing marriage rules, since the function of the totem was to identify the clan of a person and to enforce rules of endogamy and exogamy; in short, it was a logical way of enforcing the incest taboo.

The second consequence is a paradox regarding structuralism's nineteenth-century forebears. For the past hundred years, a single, powerful conception infused almost every doctrine in the social sciences. This was the idea that under the surface appearance of a world of rationality was an underlying structure of irrationality. For Marx, underneath the formally free exchange of commodities in accordance with rational self-interest lay the anarchy of the market and the reduction of men to things. For Freud, beneath the veneer of civilization (the social superego) was the turbulent, aggressive id. For Pareto, under the logical system of thought were the residues of sentiment. For Max Weber, under the rational calculation of means to ends was a functionalized world where the means became the ends in themselves. It was this convergence, if not consensus, which gave force to the apprehension about the nature of man and the fragile character of society.

But in the view of Lévi-Strauss and Piaget (and Noam Chomsky), behind the disorder and the flux of the world, beneath the large varieties of culture and the extraordinary number of languages, is a substructure of rationality and order. The common source is the character of linguistics and the properties of mind. For Chomsky, mind has the innate power to generalize rules, while language itself, grammar and syntax, has a set of properties embedded in deep structures which can be intuited and generalized by the mind. For Lévi-Strauss, what defines culture is the ability of mind to make necessary, logical distinctions; beneath the wide range of social relations are a limited number of cross-ties, while, despite the diversity of cultures, there is a limited set of invariant forms that can be deciphered and made intelligible by transformational rules.

If this is so, it is in a crucial respect a return to Kant. For Kant, philosophy was the imposition of logical order on factual disorder. Knowledge is not the "orders of fact," which can never be verified, but the "matters of relations," and these relations themselves, the categories we use to organize experience, are innate properties of mind.

6. *The tendency to Formalism.* Within anthropology, it was Radcliffe-Brown who argued that structure is of the order of fact, derived from the observation of each particular society. Anthropology, then, could be a natural science built up from induction. But for Lévi-Strauss, such an effort is hopeless, for it cannot map the variety of order or reduce it to manageable proportions. For Lévi-Strauss, social structure "has nothing to do with empirical reality but with the models which are built up after it." What the anthropologist does is to elaborate a language "and to account with a small number of rules for phenomena held until then to be entirely different. Thus in the absence of an inaccessible factual truth, we [arrive] at a truth of reason." In effect, structuralist thought consists not in identifying a recurrent content under a variety of literary forms but "in perceiving invariant forms within different contexts."[20] In an essay on the Slavic linguist Vladimir Propp, Lévi-Strauss denies the charge. He writes: "Contrary to formalism, structuralism refuses to set the concrete against the abstract. . . . *Form* is defined by opposition to material other than itself. But *structure* has no distinct content; it is content itself, apprehended in a logical organization conceived as property of the real."[21] But this begs the question for Lévi-Strauss insists that a myth can never be properly understood by its *manifest* content but by the *imputed* relations, or homologies, established by the analyst.

In this regard, Lévi-Strauss is following the logic of Roman Jakobson and his associates in the so-called Prague School of Linguistics, who searched for the basic building blocks of language in the units of sound (phonemes), and who postulated a small set of distinctive features required to produce a sound which would account exhaustively for all sounds used in the languages of the world. In his study of kinship, which anthropology takes to be the fundamental unit of social organization, Lévi-Strauss reduced all the multitudinous systems and elaborate rules to three structures and two forms of exchange, each dependent on a single differential, the harmonic or disharmonic character of a given regime. All principles of kinship came down to relations between rules of residence and rules of descent.

In these areas, and later, more extensively, in his analysis of myth, Lévi-Strauss makes the fundamental argument that the content of any relationship is idiosyncratic, and what is crucial is the structure of the relationship itself. Once these structures are identified, the anthropologist can seek for the transformation rules that would allow him to identify the limited number of forms under which the relations could be subsumed.

It would be exhausting and far beyond my limitations of space to go into the specifics of the work of men as prolific as Piaget, who has written or collaborated on more than fifty books and hundreds of articles, or Lévi-Strauss, whose four volumes of *Mythologues* alone deal with several hundred myths, or Jacques Lacan, whose talent for neologism bursts the bounds of the French language itself, or Louis Althusser, the Marxist who has repudiated the early writings of Marx as Hegelian, and who rests his claim that Marxism is a science on a structuralist reading of *Das Kapital*—let alone into the linguistic sources of their works, or the literary expositors who have extended the ideas of semiology into all domains.

It is not the specific content of these works that is important but the intention and reach of structuralism, which seeks to capture no less than the "dream of reason" by constructing a general theory of the human mind. In classical philosophy there was an effort to identify the first principles which would be controlling of all other distinctions in the analysis and classification of phenomena, an effort which dominated philosophy from Aristotle to Aquinas. In Descartes the dream of reason was to perfect an *organon*, a method, that would tie together the realm of abstraction with the realm of real-world space, an organon that Descartes thought he had achieved in the union of algebra and geometry that today is called analytical geometry. In the social sciences the dream of reason was the effort of Auguste Comte to find the laws of thought that would explain the stages of the human mind, from the theological to the metaphysical to the positive stage of human knowledge. Marx thought, at least in the extravagant claims made by Engels, that he could uncover the laws of social development, as Darwin had elaborated the principle of biological evolution. In contemporary sociology Talcott Parsons thought he could build a general theory of action whose four components—the organismic, the personality system, the social system, and the cultural system—could provide a complete morphology of social relations. Structuralism is the latest and, in some ways, the most ambitious of these efforts.

One of the reasons why structuralism has been somewhat alien to Anglo-American thought is that the English tradition of philosophy, the dominant weight until recent years, has been one of skepticism, of empiricism, and, especially under the influence of Russell, of *analysis* in which the intention of philosophy is to clarify meaning by clarifying terms through an examination of the way words work in sentences. But even there one comes up against the wall of the later Wittgenstein, who insisted that there is no constitutive correlation between our language and the world it is supposed to denote, select, reflect, and that we cannot establish an isomorphic relation between words and what they refer to. One accepts rules as conventions, but rules are constructed and can be changed.

Structuralism is really a *logique* in which the model is mathematics, and like mathematics it is less interested in content than in relations (just as algebra replaces numbers with symbols to make the relations more manipulable) and in the combinatorial modes which expand the number of relations. In its method, structuralism follows the logic of set theory, in which elements and transformations are placed in formal mathematical terms. Piaget, in particular, has been influenced by the Bourbaki (a fictitious name given to a circle of French mathematicians), who have been collectively publishing an encyclopedic work on basic mathematical structures which seeks to axiomatize all mathematical propositions. Piaget has also suggested, in his essay on Psychology in the UNESCO volume, that it is pointless to distinguish between social logic (inter-individual or collective actions) and individual logic since both are governed by common logico-mathematical structures (p. 246). And Lévi-Strauss in his *Elementary Structures of Kinship* has argued that "the laws of thought, primitive or civilized, are the same as those which find expression in physical reality and in social reality, which is simply one of their aspects." For Piaget, just as there is a congruence between mathematics and physical reality, there is the congruence of mathematics, language, and the structure of human thought.

What is one to make of all this? Is it a Library of Babel which, in the image of Borges, is "limitless and periodic," so that "if an external voyager were to traverse it in any direction, he would find, after many centuries, that the same volumes are repeated in the same disorder (which, repeated, would constitute an order: Order itself)"? Or is it a new *organon*, the key to the deciphering of knowledge?

For Lévi-Strauss, his conclusions are not "factual truths" but the "truths of reason." This very rationalism by reduction is the heart of one of the arguments about the validity of the argument. Sociological relativists reject the idea of an emergent human nature. Functionalists do not accept the proposition that the coherence of culture lies in some analogical structures rather than in the actual interdependencies of daily life. Materialists scorn the mentalistic approach, while evolutionists and humanists (each in a different way and for different reasons) may see a principle of "emergence" in human powers or in the nature of consciousness that is not captured in the logical sets of combinatorial mathematics.

There are other questions. When Lévi-Strauss breaks apart the Oedipus story and shows its homologous relationship to myths in cultures far removed, or when Edmund Leach, in an ingenious structuralist interpretation of Genesis and other stories in the Bible (the Abraham/Isaac story and the Jephthah/daughter story in Judges), shows, by "transformation rules" (God is changed to Father, virgin son to virgin daughter), that the stories are binary opposites, is one deciphering a code or *imposing* a code on these stories? How does one judge? Like serial music, it may only be a matter of ingenious recombination.

There is, perhaps, a different aspect to these efforts, which goes to the heart of the question whether the social sciences can become closed systems on the model of the natural sciences, or whether they remain bound to the humanistic disciplines, with their emphasis on the diversity of human responses and the variety of meanings which constitute the richness of the human imagination. Perhaps there is a way to thread this argument: it is to say that there *are* cultural universals but that these universals are not the underlying formal patterns or structures of action but the existential predicaments that confront all human beings and all human groups in the consciousness of their days. One can say that all human groups respond to some modal situations: the fact of death, the character of tragedy, the nature of love, the definition of courage, the idea of reciprocity, and the like. The *responsa* they give is the *history* of human culture, in all its variety, but in the essential understanding of life, the questions are recurrent and always the same.

---

[1] Ruth Benedict, *Patterns of Culture* (Boston: Houghton Mifflin, 1934), pp. 12, 13–14, 15.

[2] Ernst Mayr, "Evolution," *Scientific American*, September 1978, pp. 52–53.

[3] E. O. Wilson, "Biology and the Social Sciences," *Daedalus*, Fall 1977, p. 137; emphasis added.

[4] I take the example from a summary of a workshop discussion on Sociobiology and the Social Sciences held by the American Academy of Arts and Sciences, March and April, 1977.

[5] "The Intellectual Gantry of Neoclassical Economic Policy," chap. 2 in William Breit and Roger L. Ransom, *The Academic Scribblers* (New York: Holt, Rinehart and Winston, 1971), p. 14. I have profited as well from the review "Monetarism: A Historic-Theoretic Perspective," by A. Robert Nobay and Harry G. Johnson, *The Journal of Economic Literature*, June 1977.

[6] Robert M. Solow, "What We Know and Don't Know About Inflation," M.I.T. *Technology Review*, December 1978/January 1979, p. 38. Mr. Solow's witty account is recommended for the story of his adventures with the Phillips Curve.

[7] Lester C. Thurow, "Economics 1977," *Daedalus*, Fall 1977, pp. 83–84.

[8] On the literature on monetarism, *see* the essay by Nobay and Johnson, op. cit. Milton Friedman's theories are put forth in *Studies in the Quantity Theory of Money* (University of Chicago Press, 1956), and his Presidential Address, "The Role of Monetary Policy," *American Economic Review*, March 1968. The essays by Robert Lucas that brought attention to his theories are "Expectations and the Neutrality of Money," *Journal of Economic Theory*, April 1972, and "Understanding Business Cycles," Supplement to *Journal of Monetary Economics*, 1977. In addition to the fine exposition in the 1977 Annual Report of the Federal Reserve Bank of Minneapolis, there is a popular but oversimplified account of the "Rational Expectations" school in "The New Down-to-Earth Economics," *Fortune*, Dec. 31, 1978.

[9] Basil J. Moore, "A Post-Keynesian Approach to Monetary Theory," *Challenge*, September/October 1978, p. 52. For an overview of the subject, *see* Alfred S. Eichner and J. A. Kregel, "An Essay on Post-Keynesian Theory: A New Paradigm in Economics," *Journal of Economic Literature*,

December 1975. Also, Michal Kalecki, *Selected Essays on the Dynamics of the Capitalist Economy, 1933–1970* (Cambridge University Press, 1971); Joan Robinson, *Essays in the Theory of Economic Growth* (London: Macmillan, 1962); Alfred S. Eichner, *The Megacorp and Oligopoly* (Cambridge University Press, 1976).

[10] Assar Lindbeck, "Stabilization Policy in Open Economies with Endogenous Politicians," *American Economic Review*, May 1976, p. 18.

[11] Daniel Bell, *The Coming of Post-Industrial Society* (New York: Basic Books, 1973), p. 279.

[12] *The Journal of Law and Economics*, April 1977, p. 2.

[13] For Simon's major work, see *Adminstrative Behavior*, 3rd ed. (New York: Free Press, 1976, expanded with a new Introduction); *The New Science of Management Decision* (Englewood Cliffs, N. J.: Prentice-Hall, 1977); *Models of Man* (New York: John Wiley, 1957). Of the technical papers, the two most apropos are: "Theories of Bounded Rationality," in C. B. McGuire and Roy Radner (eds.), *Decision and Organization* (Amsterdam: North-Holland Publishing Co., 1972), and "From Substantive to Procedural Rationality," in S. J. Latsis (ed.), *Method and Appraisal in Economics* (Cambridge: Cambridge University Press, 1976).

[14] For a discussion of these questions, *see* my essay, "The Once and Future Marx," in the *American Journal of Sociology* (vol. 83, no. 1, July 1977), reprinted in my book, *The Winding Passage: Essays and Sociological Journeys, 1960–1980* (Cambridge, Mass.: Abt Books, 1980).

[15] Jürgen Habermas, *Toward a Rational Society* (Boston: Beacon Press, 1970), p. 104.

[16] George Lichtheim, "Sartre, Marxism, and History," in *Collected Essays* (New York: Viking Press, 1973) p. 378.

[17] Jean Piaget, "General Problems of Inter-disciplinary Research and Common Mechanisms," in *Main Trends of Research in the Social and Human Sciences: Part One: Social Sciences* (Mouton/Unesco; Paris, The Hague: 1970), p. 479.

[18] Howard Gardner, *The Quest for Mind* (New York: Alfred A. Knopf, 1973), pp. 9–10.

[19] *The Structuralists: From Marx to Lévi-Strauss*, edited by Richard T. and Fernande M. De George (New York: Anchor Books, Doubleday & Co., 1972).

[20] *Structural Anthropology*, vol. II (New York: Basic Books, 1976), p. 21.

[21] Ibid., p. 115.